How to Win a Startup Pitch Competition

Successful Insights from a
Topnotch Judge for Boosting Your Startup

Dr. Lance B. Eliot, MBA, PhD

Disclaimer: This book is presented solely for educational and entertainment purposes. The author and publisher are not offering it as legal, accounting, or other professional services advice. The author and publisher make no representations or warranties of any kind and assume no liabilities of any kind with respect to the accuracy or completeness of the contents and specifically disclaim any implied warranties of merchantability or fitness of use for a particular purpose. Neither the author nor the publisher shall be held liable or responsible to any person or entity with respect to any loss or incidental or consequential damages caused, or alleged to have been caused, directly or indirectly, by the information or programs contained herein. Every company is different and the advice and strategies contained herein may not be suitable for your situation.

DEDICATION

To my wonderful daughter, Lauren, and my wonderful son, Michael.

Carthago delenda est (from Ancient Rome; absolutely support your ideas).

CONTENTS

Acknowledgments iii
Introduction 1

Part 1: About Startup Pitch Competitions

1 Why do a Startup Pitch Competition 11
2 What Happens at a Startup Pitch Competition 31
3 The Pitch Judges and How They Think 43
4 Use the LBE Scorecard as Your Guide 55
5 Self-Diagnosing Your Startup Via LBE Scorecard 69
6 Falsehoods about Your Pitch Approach 77

Part II: Understanding the LBE Scorecard

L1   The Solvable Problem...................................... 87
L2   The Viable Solution 91
L3   The Customers 95
L4   This Is Similar To.. 99
L5   Core Business Model 103
L6   Product/Service 107
L7   Differentiation 111
L8   Startup Funding 115
L9   Monetization 119
L10 Unfair Advantage 123
L11 About the Presenter 127
L12 About the Team 131
L13 Accomplished To-Date 135
L14 The Ask 139
L15 Cost Structure 143
L16 Exit Strategy 147
L17 Marketing 151
L18 Competitors 155
L19 Prior Pitches 159
L20 The Pitch 163

Conclusion & Final Advice 167
Appendix A: Teaching with this Material 171
About the Author 185
Addendum 186

Lance B. Eliot

ACKNOWLEDGMENTS

As a successful entrepreneur, I have been the beneficiary of advice and counsel by many friends, colleagues, family, investors, and many others. I want to thank everyone that has aided me throughout my career. I write from the heart and the head about starting up a business, having experienced first-hand what it means to have others around you that support you during the good times and the tough times.

To Warren Bennis, one of the greats on leadership and my doctoral advisor and ultimately a colleague, I offer my deepest thanks and appreciation, especially for his calm and insightful wisdom and support.

To Mark Stevens and his generous efforts toward entrepreneurship including funding and supporting the USC Stevens Center for Innovation.

To Lloyd Greif and the USC Lloyd Greif Center for Entrepreneurial Studies for their ongoing encouragement of founders and entrepreneurs.

To James Bottom and his Herculean efforts at the USC LaunchPad.

To Kaustav Chaudhuri (K.C.) and his Pitch Globally and his The Wise Founder for the ongoing efforts of enhancing the startup ecosystem.

To Derek Anderson, founder of Startup Grind for his courage in building such a vast network to encourage startups.

To Cody Simms, Executive Director of the Americas at Techstars, and the incredible team that each day is mentoring and supporting startups.

To Peter Drucker, William Wang, Aaron Levie, Peter Kim, Jon Kraft, Cindy Crawford, Jenny Ming, Steve Milligan, Chis Underwood, Frank Gehry, and Colonel Sanders, Buzz Aldrin, Steve Forbes, Bill Thompson, Dave Dillon, Alan Fuerstman, Larry Ellison, Jim Sinegal, John Sperling, Mark Stevenson, Anand Nallathambi, Thomas Barrack, Jr., and many other business founders and leaders that I have met and gained mightily from doing so.

Thanks to Ed Trainor, Kevin Anderson, James Hickey, Wendell Jones, Ken Harris, DuWayne Peterson, Mike Brown, Jim Thornton, Abhi Beniwal, Al Biland, John Nomura, and many others for their unwavering support during my business career.

And most of all thanks as always to Lauren and Michael, for their ongoing support and for having seen me writing and heard much of this material during the many months involved in writing it. To their patience and willingness to listen.

Lance B. Eliot

INTRODUCTION

This is a book about how to win a startup pitch competition. Congratulations that you presumably have a startup that you want to consider pitching at a competition. This is a wise move. Furthermore, I applaud you that you want to try and prepare for giving a pitch. As a seasoned judge at startup pitch competitions, I see over and over that many of the startups do inadequate preparation. They just blindly show-up and hope for the best.

Unfortunately for them, they have entered into the lion's den without a chair and a whip. Their lack of preparation shows itself right away. The judges give them a low score, and they often are taken aback that they did not win. They are clueless as to why they did not win. There usually is nothing told to the "losers" other than that they did not win. As you will see in this book, there are lots of "wins" to be had at a competition that aren't only about winning the grand prize. The contacts you make, the experience you gain, are all crucial on the road toward getting your startup flying.

You will undoubtedly be making many pitches during the timeline of your startup. You will likely need to make pitches to investors that have directly been willing to meet you. You will need to make pitches to potential mentors or advisers. You might need to make pitches to potential business partners such as suppliers or vendors that you are wanting to involve in your startup. By having done startup pitch competitions, you will be ready to woo the investors. There might also be investors at the startup pitch competition, though in that case they are looking at all of the participants and you will be one of many being assessed.

I often tell founders a story which the founder of Pandora told me. He indicated that they pitched Pandora over 250 times. My hope is to provide you in this book with enough insights and techniques that you will get to a yes before having to do 250 pitches, and furthermore that your odds of winning a startup pitch competition will be heightened.

1

As they say, there are no guarantees in life. Your startup might flounder and flop. It happens a lot. For every Facebook or Snapchat that makes it big, I assure you there are hundreds and even thousands of startups that never got off the ground. I don't want you to be discouraged. I know that my comments about the failure rate of startups seems gloomy. Just want you to know that by pursuing a startup, you are taking a risky road that has low odds. If you are in the place and position that you can take the chance, I say go for it.

Take a look at Figure 1. On the vertical access is the *Startup Vibe*, which is my way of expressing the notion that a startup will have a kind of vibe or buzz going for it. Often, it starts relatively low and builds up over time (the horizontal axis shows time). People around you get excited. You get excited. Your passion is riding high.

There usually then is a downward slump. Things aren't happening as you had hoped. The startup seems stuck. No traction. The initial excitement has worn off. People are beginning to wonder why you are still trying to get the startup going. These are the tough times.

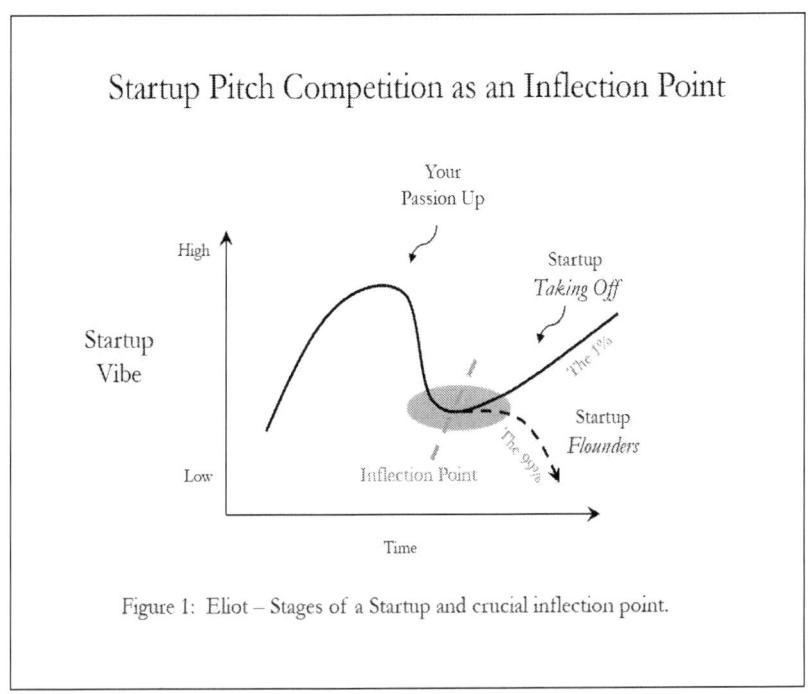

Figure 1: Eliot – Stages of a Startup and crucial inflection point.

Something has to break the downward slump. At an inflection point, you either head upward or the startup does a deeper dive. *One way to get to the inflection point involves participating in startup pitch competitions.*

Why is participating in a startup pitch competition a potential inflection point for your startup? Because many startups are done in a relative vacuum, often being conceived of, born, and initially developed <u>only</u> by the founder and some close friends, family, or colleagues. You have exhausted those resources in terms of finding ways to get your startup fully underway. There is nothing there to cause your startup to take a turn. But, a startup pitch competition could be the juice or catalyst that does so.

By participating in a startup pitch competition, you will get real-world feedback from usually seasoned startup experienced judges, and you will get feedback from other complete "strangers" at the event. I use the word "strangers" which sounds ominous, but my point is that they are people that might have ideas that you've not considered, they might have contacts that you don't have, and otherwise breath new air into your startup. These other strangers are likely to be investors, fellow entrepreneurs, professional mentors and advisers, and so on. These are people that are outside your personal bubble and so will help you to gauge where your startup is headed, doing so without necessarily worrying about hurting your feelings.

I admit that this can be both good and bad. As will be explained in this book, your participating in a startup pitch competition might dash your dreams. I believe that if you really are an earnest entrepreneur, you will look at the feedback differently. Rather than thinking that your idea of a better mousetrap can never be accomplished, you will instead realize that the mousetrap you envision is say not feasible or maybe has already been done. Instead of tossing in the towel, you will consider changing or (in the popular parlance) do a "pivoting" of your business.

I ask founders all the time, would they rather spend tons of their time on something that has little chance of succeeding, or at least go and find out if it has such little chance and then pivot to something that does have better odds? I would suggest you are better off to find out as early as possible whether your dream has legs. There are founders that I know that mortgaged their house and stopped eating out, just to cover the costs of their startup. Sadly, once they discovered that startup was aimed the wrong direction, they had already consumed what little of their own self-funding that they had. This funding is often referred to as bootstrapping your startup.

If you participate in a startup pitch competition, you will likely find out whether your bootstrap is being spent wisely. The cost to participate in a pitch competition is relatively low. It is frankly overly easy to participate. I will explain in this book what happens and the steps involved. I will also explain how to prepare yourself for the competition. This includes tips of what it takes to win.

Am I saying that you should tomorrow rush over to a startup pitch competition and get in? No! As explained in this book, you want to do so when the time is right and when you are prepared. If you follow the suggestions in this book, you will have a clear notion of what needs to be done in preparation. Think of this book as arming you with the chair and whip to enter into the lion's den that I alluded to earlier.

I also ask you to consider this book in a light differently than you might have thought initially. This is not solely about wanting to win a startup pitch competition. Winning such a competition is small in comparison to making sure that your startup is in good shape and primed for success.

Generally, startups that are in good shape and that are primed for success are the winners at these competitions. In essence, winning doesn't make your startup good per se, it is because it is good that you are able to win. See the logic?

What does it take to win a startup pitch competition? A well-shaped startup, which I will define for you when I explain the scorecards used by judges and how they think. They know a good startup when they see one. You will see the kinds of factors and elements that go into that gestalt. Speaking of gestalt, which is a general sense of looking at something as a whole rather than focusing only on its individual parts, look at Figure 2.

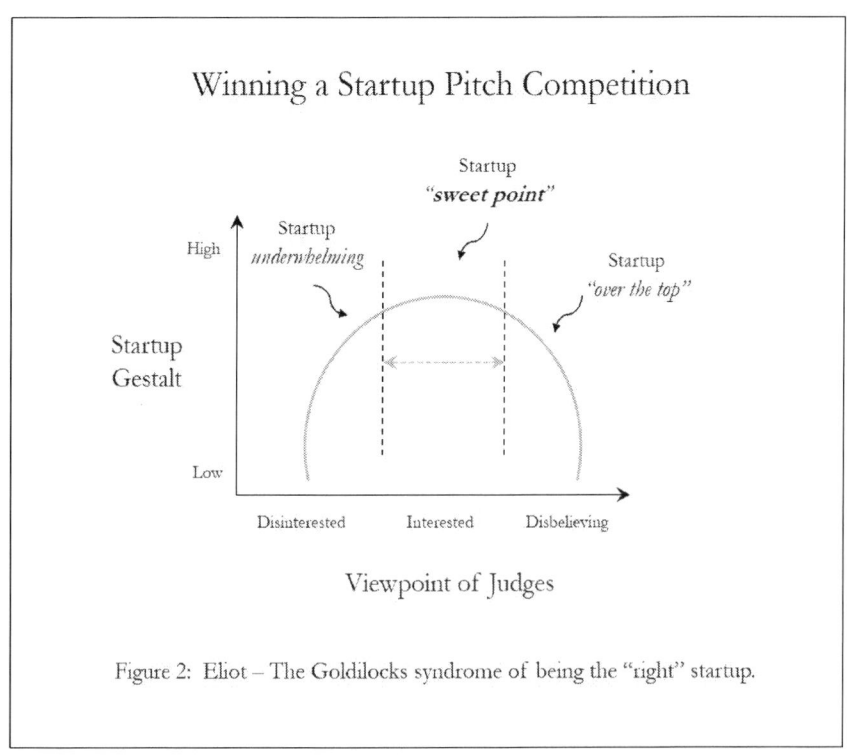

Figure 2: Eliot – The Goldilocks syndrome of being the "right" startup.

The vertical axis has a ***Startup Gestalt***, and the horizontal axis is the viewpoint of the judges. There is an inverted U-shape curve shown. By default, your startup is considered underwhelming in that judges see the same startups over and over again.

You might think your startup is wholly original, but I assure you that whatever you have come up with, probably someone else is thinking about it too. One popular line that might surprise you is that ideas are considered cheap in startups, and that it is the execution of bringing the startup to existence that is the hard part. This is why those entrepreneurs that think they are "safer" to not tell anyone about their startup, lest someone will steal their idea, are shocked when they discover that stealing someone else's idea does not happen as much as you assume.

When you go to participate a startup pitch competition, you will likely recognize many aspects of your startup. Of course, if you really have invented a new surgical device that no one else has ever seen, or created a new kind of fruit snack that will solve world hunger, I do say protect those as soon as you can, via some kind of Intellectual Property (IP) protection or whatever else makes sense. But these are rarities.

Telling others about the underlying concept and ideas of your startup are not likely to mean that someone else will go out tomorrow and do what your startup is doing. It can happen, but not often. You will more likely benefit from telling others about it, getting their feedback and maybe spreading the word, so that attention comes to you and you can push along your startup more readily.

Back to the Figure 2. You gestalt is low when the judges are disinterested because the startup is underwhelming. Your gestalt is also low if your startup is some harebrained notion that there just does not seem to be any sensible way it could work. That takes you to the right hand side of the inverted U-shape. The judges are in strong disbelief. My favorite example was a pitch by a founder that said he was going to replace Facebook. He was serious. The judges leaned back in their chairs, and assumed we would be blown away by some incredible revelation. He basically explained Facebook and said that's what his startup was going to do. Sigh.

Your startup will need to be in the upper middle area of the inverted U-shape. It is a startup that is credible, has something fresh to it, does not go over the top, and that you as the founder can appropriately articulate. The pitch is equally as important as the startup, which I emphasize because the pitch informs the judges about the startup. A lousy pitch makes it hard for the judges to know what your startup might really have as merits.

WHAT THIS BOOK PROVIDES

What does this book provide to you? Lots of important and useful aspects about how to assess your startup. Gobs of background info about what happens at a startup pitch competition. A plethora of suggestions and recommendations for how to get the most benefit of participating and indications of what it takes to win. *And most importantly a practical, usable scorecard that reflects what your startup needs to have as its elements and a scoring approach to gauge how you are doing.*

Let's do a quick tour of the book.

In Chapter 1, we will look at the reasons for participating in a startup pitch competition. You ought to know why it is a good idea to participate. I also explain why some founders don't participate. From this, you can decide what you want to do.

In Chapter 2, I explain in detail what happens at startup pitch competitions. This will ensure that you are aware of what will take place and so you won't get caught unawares if you participate. Not all of the pitch competitions are exactly the same, but there is a general structure and approach that is common to most of them.

In Chapter 3, we cover the inner mindset of the judges. This will guide you toward preparing your pitch. Knowing how judges think is important, since otherwise you will perform like most pitches that I see, whereby the founder talks about what they care about, which is not necessarily what the judges care about.

For example, had an expert on automobiles that used his entire pitch time to explain the intricacies of how a fuel injector works and how "bad" the prevailing versions are. We never learned what his proposed solution was, nor what his startup does, nor what funding he might have gotten, nor who was on his team, etc. He might have built the greatest new fuel injector ever, but all we knew was that we knew next to nothing about his startup. He scored toward the bottom (yes, there were some even worse than him!).

In Chapter 4, and speaking of scores, judges often use a scorecard, so I provide to you a "long form" version that is very comprehensive. I also provide a "short form" version that is lighter. By seeing what judges use as scoring, you can prepare your startup and your pitch accordingly.

In Chapter 5, I urge you to use the scorecard to do a self-diagnosis of your startup. It will help you to improve your startup, regardless of whether you ever participate in a startup pitch competition.

In Chapter 6, I cover various falsehoods that others will tell you about as advice on how to do your pitch. Though these falsehoods are usually told in sincerity of trying to help you, unfortunately the falsehoods can actually make your pitch worse, if you abide by them.

The second part of the book is an indication of each of the elements of the scorecard. This will provide you with added detail of what you should be doing in each of the elements.

WHY THIS BOOK

I have seen literally hundreds of startups by being a judge at many, many startup pitch competitions. I am also a serial entrepreneur that has started startups, and run them, and sold them. I have made pitches. I can say that I have been in the shoes of the participants at the startup pitch competitions.

As such, I see founders that come up to pitch and they have no clue as to what a business consists of. They are experts in something else, whether it is technology, or cars, or medicine, etc., and they are wanting to turn their expertise into a product or service, which they realize they need a business in order to do.

In this book, I provide a business startup perspective that I hope will help those budding entrepreneurs. I have taught courses on entrepreneurship, and I was a volunteer counselor for the Small Business Administration (SBA). I have been a mentor to startups and an angel investor. I have tried to wrap a lot of those insights into this book.

At pitch competitions, not only do some founders not have a foundation about what a startup should consist of, they also are not able to properly pitch their startup. I hope that this book will help them to understand what a pitch should cover and how to best perform the pitch.

For founders that are thinking about doing a startup, use this material to help you consider what the startup needs to contain and ultimately how you will pitch it.

For founders that already have a startup, use this material to assess where you are at and what you need to enhance. If you have not yet done a startup pitch competition, this will spark you to consider doing so.

For founders that have a startup and have made pitches, this material will seem likely familiar, but I am betting that it will have nonetheless some new "Aha!" moments for you. It will increase your odds of winning, I would hope.

For researchers that study entrepreneurship, you likely know that the amount of substantive research on this specific topic is relatively light. We need more studies and deeper research to be done. I truly hope that this book will inspire you to do so.

For students studying business and especially startups or founders, the topic of startup pitch competitions is not especially covered in your classes. When it is covered, it is just an aside. This book makes up for that deficiency in your diet.

For all readers, I hope that you will find the material in this book to be stimulating. Some of it will be repetitive of things you already know. But I am pretty sure that you'll also find various eureka moments whereby you'll discover a new technique or approach that you had not earlier thought of. I am also betting that there will be material that forces you to rethink some of your current practices.

I am not saying you will suddenly have an epiphany and change what you are doing. I do think though that you will reconsider or perhaps retune what you are doing.

For anyone choosing to use this book for teaching purposes, please take a look at my suggestions for doing so, as described in the Appendix. I have found the material handy in courses that I have taught, and likewise other faculty have told me that they have found the material handy, in some cases as extended readings and in other instances as a core part of their course (depending on the nature of the class).

In my writing for this book, I have tried carefully to blend both the practitioner and the academic styles of writing. It is not as dense as is typical academic journal writing, but at the same time offers depth by going into the nuances and trade-offs of various practices.

The word "deep" is in vogue today, meaning getting deeply into a subject or topic, and so is the word "unpack" which means to tease out the underlying aspects of a subject or topic. I have sought to offer material that addresses an issue or topic by going relatively deeply into it and make sure that it is well unpacked.

YOUR STARTUP AND YOUR PITCH

I admit that I have a fondness for startups and those that want to undertake them. I have worked in large, billion dollar sized firms. They are great. On the other hand, there is something about taking an idea, creating a startup business around it, reshaping it, growing it, and seeing it succeed. I know that the odds of any small business succeeding is low. The statistics show that few make it past the first year.

Maybe it is the maverick in me. The survivalist. The desire to start something and see it blossom. Whatever it is, I want to transfer what I know to you. I want your startup to be successful. I want to be sitting there as a judge, and realize that your startup has what it takes to make it. Your pitch conveys what a great startup you have. That's my goal for writing this book.

Please use what you can, and I wish you the best of luck in your endeavors!

.

CHAPTER 1

WHY DO A STARTUP PITCH COMPETITION

CHAPTER 1

WHY DO A STARTUP PITCH COMPETITION

PREFACE

In this chapter, I explore the reasons that you should consider participating in a startup pitch competition. Notice that I say "participating" and did not use the word "competing" when describing your efforts at a startup pitch competition. You are certainly going to be competing, and that's the overt basis for being there. As will be revealed in this chapter, these startup pitch competitions are not merely about competing to win. You are also going to find other very valuable aspects of being in the competition.

You should strive to win the startup pitch competition, and so I do urge you to be highly competitive and be thinking of yourself as competing for the prize. At the same time, I urge you to think of yourself as "participating" which maybe will open your eyes to the other takeaways that can be had. As an active participant, you will have an opportunity to hobnob with fellow attendees and other participants. You will get a moment in the sun to show who you are and what your startup is about. You will find it rewarding in many ways, regardless of whether you actually win that particular pitch competition. If you think of yourself solely as "competing" you are bound to cut yourself off from all of those other valuable aspects and be so myopic that the only thing you do is compete. Not only would not winning be a blow, but you would have gotten nothing else out of the experience. That's a real loss to you and your startup.

———

CHAPTER 1:
WHY DO A STARTUP PITCH COMPETITION

What should a startup be doing to try and ensure that it will grow into a viable business? There are lots of answers to that question. Some would say that you need to do inner soul searching and ascertain whether you really have the "right stuff" to be an entrepreneur. Some say that you should be getting educated on how to start and bring to fruition a new business. Some say that funding is king, and so you should be talking to everyone that has a buck that could be invested into your startup.

Those answers are all certainly reasonably sound ways to proceed with getting your startup underway. One additional answer, and that is the focus of this book is that you should consider participating in a startup pitch competition. Yes, I am a big proponent of taking a shot at boosting your startup by participating in a startup pitch competition. And, not just doing so one time, but I say that you should consider doing several, depending upon your circumstances and what stage your startup is at (which we'll be covering a bit later on).

Now, some might think that I am saying that you should participate in a startup competition "no matter what" – but that's not what I am saying. There is a right timing, right place, and right way to participate in a startup pitch competition. If you aren't ready for it, I say in the loudest terms "Don't do it!" (you could do more harm than good). Only participate when the situation is ripe.

LOTS OF STARTUP PITCH COMPETITIONS

Keep in mind that startup competitions are running all the time. I say this so that you won't think that maybe you had better be ready for one special moment of the year. It used to be that there were only a few competitions, and if you didn't go there, you were out of luck. It was like race horsing and if the Kentucky Derby was the only real horse race to be in. You had to toil all year long, dreading the one-shot chance, and even at times be idle simply because you were waiting for the competition to then spark your startup into its next stage of growth.

You can breathe a sigh of relief. There are tons of startup pitch competitions nowadays. Small ones, big ones, ones with a specific focus like say medical device startups or social media focused startups, and so on. It is amazing how many there are. Some are done by a governmental agency, sometimes at the local city and county level, sometimes at the state and federal levels. Some are done by incubators and accelerators. Many are being done by universities and colleges. Companies are doing them, though usually more of sponsoring such a competition, but anyway you can readily do a search on-line and find a bevy of startup pitch competitions which are running all throughout the year.

LIKE A BEAUTY CONTEST

In the next chapter we'll cover the details of what happens at a startup competition. For now, it is sufficient to know that the overall notion is that startup businesses come to make a pitch and a panel of judges decides who the winner of the competition is. This notion might seem vaguely familiar to you, likely, since it give the impression of being a beauty contest. It is.

The difference here is that the "beauty" is you and your startup. Just like a beauty contest, you will need to strut your stuff in front of judges. The judges have seen lots of beauties before, and many previously were in beauty contests. Or, in other words, the judges have had startups and likely also participated in startup pitch competitions, and they now are asked to help identify the "best" of the startups at the competition.

Before a beauty contest gets underway, can you know for sure who the winner will be? Usually not. There are bound to be some that you can quickly gauge as not going to win. There is some obvious criteria that you can use to rule them out. At the same time, there are often lots of potential winners and it can be very hard to discern which will be the final winner of the competition. Same with the startup pitch competitions. There are some startups that show-up and are DOA (Dead on Arrival), while there are others that look locked-and-loaded and have a good chance of winning. We will in later chapters go over the criteria used in these startup pitch "beauty contests" so that you can be well prepared to win.

In the preface to this chapter, I emphasized that you should consider participating in a startup pitch competition, and belabored the point that I am using the word "participating" instead of the word "competing" when I make that statement. As stated, if you go into this by only thinking of competing then you are likely to be so heads-down that you will miss the bigger picture. Furthermore, if you don't win the competition, you will be entirely crushed because you put your whole basis for going on winning. Sure, if you can win it, that's the biggest goal. I can tell you though that your odds of winning for going to be low. You might find this shocking, and you are saying to yourself, hey, Lance, you don't know about your startup and how tremendous it is. Well, I am sorry to tell you that no matter how good it is, it still might be the winner. We will see why that could happen.

For now, let's focus on why you would want to participate in a startup pitch competition. To think about this topic, please take a look at Figure 1. You can see that I have listed a dozen reasons for you to participate in a pitch competition. I could have listed even more reasons. The dozen are sufficient to get across the broad range of benefits by participating. As a side note, I did say "compete" in Figure 1 and did so to get your competitive juices flowing.

Reasons to compete in a Startup Pitch Competition

	Common Reasons for doing a Pitch Competition
1	Find investors that will fund your startup
2	Get attention to your startup
3	Win prize money for your startup
4	Seek and obtain a mentor for your startup
5	Received free feedback about your startup
6	Spark a potential pivot to help your startup
7	Allow you to put a stake in the ground
8	Validate your startup as something viable
9	Connect with peer entrepreneurs
10	Make contacts that can help your startup
11	Gauge your competition and what is hot and not
12	Serve as your moment of truth

Figure 1: Eliot - Reasons to compete in a Startup Pitch Competition.

Let's take a closer look at each of the dozen reasons. I want to provide you with added insights so that you can make sure to leverage these various benefits. They won't just fall into your lap. It is your job while at the startup pitch competition to glean as much as you can from it. The organizers of the event aren't necessarily going to walk you through what you need to be doing. They assume you have come to compete, and it is up to you to derive whatever else you can from the event.

I can always spot the savvy participants because I see them doing what they can to maximize the value of the event. They usually figured it out on their own by having repeatedly come to such events. I hope here that I can get you up-to-speed right away.

Find investors that will fund your startup

One of the most popular reasons to participate in a startup pitch competition is to attract funding from investors. Normally, you might not know many investors, or know investors that don't have enough money to bankroll your startup, or investors that are skittish and unsure about your startup. In which case, you need to expand your horizon and find other investors that are interested in you and your startup. How can you find such investors? By participating in a startup pitch competition. There are usually flocks of investors at these events

Be aware that everyone at a startup pitch event can either be an investor or have contacts with investors. I mention this because when you are hobnobbing, sometimes founders instantly ask if a person is an investor, and if not then the founder turns away from the person and goes to the next. There are bound to be attendees that aren't investors but that know investors and can connect you accordingly. Treating such connectors rudely won't do you much good.

Also, the grapevine about who is a "good" investor versus a "bad" investor is important to get plugged into. Some investors will tie so many conditions to the funding that it will clog up your business, and some will be so overbearing that you will spend most of your time with the investor and little time on your actual startup. Find out the real skinny about the investors and keep your eyes open. Not all investors are equal and not all investments are worth accepting for your startup.

Get attention to your startup

Probably the next most common reason to attend a startup pitch competition is to get attention to your startup. If you have been laboring away in your garage, or spare bedroom, or dorm room, it is time to get out there and get your startup noticed. Even if you are posting on social media about your startup, you still will find it valuable to meet other startup stakeholders in-person. They will potentially help to spread your message.

Usually, these pitch events have attendees that are all looking for the next great thing. They want to find something that is going to hit it big. The organizers certainly hope so, since it would help the branding of their events. Other attendees would like to say they were there when the next Facebook was first presented. You should come prepared to tout your startup. Bring business cards, bring any brochures or samples or whatever you can to show that your startup is tangible and real. Imaginary startups will get some attention, but as they say "ideas are cheap" and an indication of actual progress and action will help boost your chances of gaining attention.

Win prize money for your startup

This is one of the most obvious reasons to participate in a startup pitch competition. There is often a monetary prize involved. It can be very modest, like a $100 to $1000, and it can be larger, like $10,000 or more. The odds are that it won't be enough money to dramatically impact your business and so thinking of the event as solely to win the prize money is not very prudent. Leveraging the win by touting that your startup won the competition is likely to do more for your fledgling business. Investors and other stakeholders want to join the bandwagon of a winner, and so you can ride that kind of wave by telling the world if you win a competition.

Even if there is no prize money at all, being the winner nonetheless still allows you to brag that you were the winner, doing so to potential investors, mentors, advisers, and the like. You can also include it as part of your promotion and marketing of your firm. So, don't be dissuaded if there isn't any prize money, the winning alone can be used to your advantage.

There is also the prize that is valued in dollars but not actually dollars handed out. For example, some competitions will say that the winner gets a free consultation with one of the judges or some other mentor. This could be easily worth hundreds of dollars or even thousands, since if you paid that expert by the hour it would be costly. Furthermore, the value can be even considered higher too because the person may have contacts that can get you an investment of say $100,000 to $1,000,000, which is far more than any competition is likely to award straight out to the winner.

Seek and obtain a mentor for your startup

This next benefit of participating in a startup pitch competition involves the aspect that you might be able to find a mentor for your startup, doing so while at the event. If you went to the event as only an audience member, you might not have much chance of wandering into a mentor that so happened to be a fit for you and your startup. On the other hand, by participating, you will have told all the attendees about you and your business. The odds are that a potential mentor will then come up to talk with you afterward.

Suppose you don't win the competition – does this imply that any mentor there might decide to pass on talking with you? Heck no! The mentors are often looking for the non-winner that they know can be pumped up by their mentorship. The winner might already have a bunch of mentors that helped guide that startup to winning. Other mentors in the room might figure there is no place for them there. It is like being a baseball scout. The mentors are scouting for that really good pitcher or catcher that no one else has quite found as yet. The hidden gold nugget.

Received free feedback about your startup

By participating, you will be getting lots of feedback at the event. Fellow attendees will likely talk with you after your pitch. There might be mentors, advisers, investors, other startup founders, and just about anybody else interested in the topic of startups.

The judges are usually available to provide feedback too. All in all, you are getting a ton of feedback. This is something that normally might be expensive to get. Plus, if the only feedback you have so far is from family and friends, the attendees at the event are "strangers" and are more likely to be upfront with you. Your family and friends might want to support you, even if they think your business is wacky. At a startup pitch competition, usually the other attendees are not bashful and they will tell you if your startup is wacky.

Keep in mind that no matter what others say, it is not necessarily the correct advice. You are going to get some oddball feedback, for sure. Someone will tell you to scrap your startup and go live in the woods, while the next person will swear it is the next Facebook and assure you that by the end of the year you will be a billionaire. While at the event, take the free feedback with a grain of salt.

Spark a potential pivot to help your startup

Most startups pivot. They begin with a particular notion or approach, and after trying it or after getting feedback, they pivot to some other aspect. It is very likely this will happen to your startup. Even if you insist it won't, I would anyway be willing to put money on the fact that you will pivot at some point.

How do you know if you should pivot? At the event, you are bound to get feedback that might be suggesting you should pivot. You might even see other firms that are doing something that causes you to decide to do a pivot.

If you are interested in business pivots, I have written another book that covers that topic. It is entitled ***On Being a Pivot-Wise Business Leader: The Secrets of Strategic Leadership for Successful Business Pivots*** and covers key aspects of what to do when considering a business pivot. It also includes business case studies of famous firms and their leaders that have undergone pivots successful.

Allow you to put a stake in the ground

Sometimes your startup is only what you envision it to be. You have shaped it, but it still somewhat fuzzy at the edges. You have told your family and friends about it. But, somehow, it just still seems more of a dream than reality. It has not been tested by the real-world per se, since you have not gone outside your own personal sphere or protective bubble.

By participating at a startup pitch competition, you will have finally put a stake in the ground. This is your turf, you are telling these strangers. It is not just family and friends that are patting you on the back. You are now outside that protective bubble. If it can withstand scrutiny under bright lights, you will have a clearer sense as to what this startup is all about. The questions that come up will force you into having a sharper focus.

Validate your startup as something viable

Maybe you have a very clear cut indication of what your startup is about. You have a well-defined business model. You have considered numerous angles. You are ready to get going with selling refrigerators to Eskimo's. That's an old joke, namely that presumably Eskimo's living in an icy climate don't need refrigerators.

The point is that you need to get real-world feedback about the viability of your startup. Again, family and friends might all be telling you that they do want to buy a purple shoehorn that lights up in the dark. On the other hand, at the startup pitch competition, you might learn that such a market is a lot smaller than you are thinking.

Connect with peer entrepreneurs

Guess who else will be at the startup pitch competition? Lots and lots of other entrepreneurs. Your first impulse is that they are the competition and you need to stay at arm's length. At a competition, it is pretty much too late for anyone there to learn something from another startup pitch that is going to make the difference in the success of their winning the pitch competition at that particular event. They would likely need to time to recalculate their pitch and redo their model.

I am not saying spill your guts to your peers. You should though try to connect with them. Find out who they have as an investor, and who turned them down. Find out what tricks they've learned. The odds are that you'll gain a lot of insights from those conversations.

Your peer entrepreneurs can also be a relief valve. Are you the only one that is trying to get your startup underway while also getting your kids to school and having to work on your regular job for 50 hours per week? The odds are that there are peers there that are going through the same things as you. It can be comforting to know that you are not alone.

Make contacts that can help your startup

Nearly anyone at the event is bound to be a useful contact. Maybe they can't help you right now. Maybe it will be weeks from now, or months away. Get as many business cards as you can. Use social media like LinkedIn to be in touch. Try to keep the contacts fresh and active, rather than just having met the person for a handshake.

When you are asking for someone's contact info, please try to be civil and sensible. I have seen some that just collect them as though they are baseball trading cards. They don't talk with the person, and do not interact in any kind of dialogue. The odds are that doing this kind of robot-like transaction will limit the value of having that contact. The other side of that coin is don't try to tell your whole life story, and likewise hopefully the other person is savvy enough not to do the same to you.

Gauge your competition and what is hot and not

Is your startup unique? Maybe it is, but is it hot? There are fads and waves of what investors are looking for. Your startup might be too early. Or, it might be too late and others have already trampled that market. It is useful to watch closely the other pitches.

The odds are low that any startup at the pitch will be exactly like yours. In the sea of vast numbers of startups, they are many variations. By random chance, even if the event is focused on a particular theme or topic, I would still guess that your startup will be a bit different.

Either way, try and see if there are bits and pieces from the other startups that might fit for you. For example, I saw one pitch for a new frozen food, and the founder saw a pitch about the use of social media for those that are environmentally conscious people. She realized that her frozen food was made of organic elements and was basically good for the environment. She did not win the prize at the event, but she did say that she was going to add social media into her plans and appreciated hearing the other pitch.

Serve as your moment of truth

The last reason listed but not the least (all of these reasons are about equal in weight) to participate in a startup competition is due to what I call the "moment of truth" about your startup. I somewhat alluded to this notion earlier. If your startup has so far been within the realm of your own bubble, you might not have faced the truth of whether it can make the cut.

There is another aspect to this moment of truth. The odds are that if your startup is going succeed, you will need to do a lot of pitches. If you have not done any pitches to "strangers" before coming to the pitch competition, this is a great chance to see how it goes. Not just your startup, but you too. Are you able to passionately describe aptly what your startup is doing? Have you considered what your startup needs to do? These are all moment of truths about whether you and your startup are ready for prime time.

WHY DO SOME NOT PARTICIPATE

You might be thinking, hey, Lance, if the stated reasons are so good about being a participant, then why doesn't every startup come and participate in these pitch competitions? Glad that you asked me the question. Take a look at Figure 2. We will next cover the reasons why some don't participate.

Why some don't compete in a Startup Pitch Competition

	Why some don't do Pitch Competitions	Counter-argument
1	Don't know what to do, where to go, etc.	Read this book, prepare
2	Worried that their dreams will get crushed	Dreams need reality check
3	Have a fear of speaking	Practice, consider who speaks
4	Assume you will get belittled	Use criticism constructively
5	Cannot take rejection	Better grow some thick skin
6	Want to wait until their ideal pitch is ready	Good enough versus ideal
7	Figure it is a waste of time and effort	How else using time & effort
8	Concerned about the cost to compete	Costs are usually minimal

Figure 2: Eliot – Reasons why some don't compete and counter-arguments.

Don't know what to do, where to go, etc.

Answer: Read this book, prepare.

One big reason why some don't participate in a startup pitch competition is because they don't know much about it. They are unsure of what to do. They are unsure of how to prepare. They are unsure of what will happen. They are unsure of what the benefits are. It is a big mystery, and so I don't blame them for not participating.

I have already now tried to present to you an indication of the various potential benefits, so that you are now in-the-know. Plus, the remainder of this book will cover what to do to prepare and what to expect. I believe that takes this reason of the "why not participating" list for you.

Worried that their dreams will get crushed

Answer: Dreams need reality check

I talk to a lot of startup founders and they sometimes will tell me that they aren't going to a startup pitch competition because the feedback might crush their dreams. I guess I should have some sympathy for this. Nobody wants to have their dreams crushed. I get it.

But, look at it a different way. If you harbor this dream, and you don't test it in the real-world, you won't know whether the dream can come true. If the dream is unlikely to come true, maybe you should think of another dream which can come true. Meanwhile, if you were fixated on only that first dream, you might have wasted precious time in which your second dream could come true.

Dreams are made to be pivoted. Pinch yourself, wake-up, and go pitch your startup to see. I am taking this "why not participating" off your list.

Have a fear of speaking

Answer: Practice, consider who speaks

Another common qualm is that the founder has a fear of speaking. We all do, pretty much. I realize that some are more suited for public speaking than others. I also realize that speaking in some forums is easier than other forums. Many founders are often good at the technical aspects underlying their product or service, perhaps being a super star programmer or maybe a financial wizard or whatever. This does not mean they will necessarily also be a good speaker.

Plus, the forum of a startup pitch competition can be somewhat grinding. You are not just giving a prepared presentation, but also usually will need to do Q&A. The Q&A will not just be with anyone, but instead with judges that probably have years of business and startup experience. This all can be much more daunting that just speaking to the local basket weaving club.

One way to deal with the speaking fear involves taking a class or getting involved in a Toastmasters or equivalent kind of group. You are likely to still have the fear, but at least you will gain ways to overcome it. Also, speak in public settings as much as you can. How do you get to speak at Carnegie Hall? The reply is practice, practice, practice.

That being said, I know some that have tried relentlessly to improve their speaking ability and still are not very good at it. Also, it could take months or years to improve your speaking skills, which might cause a big delay in proceeding with the startup.

The problem in this context is that your startup will be poorly perceived if you cannot speak well enough to represent it. An alternative is to consider having someone else as your primary speaker, and you there as the secondary speaker. The primary speaker should preferably be someone also integral to the business. If you bring in a professional speaker, but they have nothing to do with the business, it is going to hurt more than help. The judges want to see the key members of the startup. If one of your team is good at speaking, make them the primary.

Notice that I am saying primary and indicating that you as the founder would be the secondary and still be a speaker. I mention this because if you are the founder and you have only your second-in-command speak, the judges will wonder why you aren't also talking. It will beg the question. If you narrow your part to something you can use to show your passion and your expertise, it would keep you less on-the-spot about the presenting. Whatever you opt to do, if you are doing a tag team approach to the presentation, make sure you are your fellow speaker(s) are well aligned and know who covers what.

I have seen multiple speakers for a startup that were utterly uncoordinated and repeated each other, and otherwise made themselves look like blundering idiots. The sad thing is that their startup looked really good, but the mess of a presentation made us think that the firm must also be a mess. We knocked them down because of it. Sad, since maybe it was the next Snapchat or Twitter, but we couldn't discern it from the clown-like act we saw.

By the way, one caveat about having multiple speakers, there are some pitch events that only allow one speaker per startup to present the pitch. You will then need to grapple with whom that should be. Sometimes, under that rule, they do allow during Q&A to have more than one member of the team speak, and so if that's the case then maybe have you as the founder do so during the Q&A. Indeed, make sure that you *purposely* answer a question, so that you aren't just waiting to be called upon.

I am taking this "why not participating" off your list.

Assume you get belittled

Answer: Use criticism constructively

Another reason why some say they won't do a startup pitch competition is because they might get belittled. Belittling is in the eye of the beholder. Will you get criticism leveled at you? Yes. Will you get criticism leveled at your startup? Yes. Will some judge maybe act mean and refer to you with unkind words. Yes.

I am not going to sugar coat the real-world for you. People are going to hate your startup idea. People are going to hate you. It all goes with the territory of doing a startup. Is this belittling? I suppose so. It is hard to separate yourself from your startup, and so anyone that pokes at your startup is poking at you.

All I can offer is that you will need to live with this and find a means to adapt to it. My way of doing so is to pretend that the criticism is being offered constructively. It might not have been shared in that manner, and it might have been given with foul words and finger waving. Anyway, I try to turn it into something constructive and excise the part that had emotion and anger in it.

I am taking this "why not participating" off your list.

Cannot take rejection

Answer: Better grow some thick skin

Rejection should become your favorite word. I kid you not. You are going to get more rejection than you can imagine. It will come at you from the left and the right, from above and below, from within and from the outside. You are going to be awash in rejection. This is the plight of the entrepreneur. Welcome to the neighborhood!

Many entrepreneurs come to their startup with a background in a technology or specialty, such as perhaps being a programmer or an expert in manufacturing or whatever. They are often not from the sales side of things. Sales people know about rejection. It is their livelihood. If you are a startup founder and not from sales, you perhaps have not experienced the kind of rejection that those in sales do. It can be shocking. Often reminds the founder of why they did not go into sales.

You though now are putting yourself into a sales position. You are having to be a sales person with respect to your startup. You are a sales person with respect to you, selling who you are and why you are doing this startup.

One of my favorite stories about rejection and startups is one that I got from the founder of Pandora, the now ridiculously successful music streaming service (I have now told this story maybe more times than him). When he and his co-founders were pitching Pandora, they did so around 250+ times. In other words, when referring to the notion of rejection, take a moment right now and count from one to the number two hundred and fifty. As you do so, say aloud the word "No!" as loud as you can, for every count. Imagine that long line of rejection. Yet, in the end, they got a yes. The yes led to the Pandora that we know and love today.

The rule-of-thumb that will get you through the rejection is this: <u>For every no, you are getting closer to a yes.</u>

I hope that helps you on the rejection thing. That being said, I would also say that you should not ignore the rejection. Pandora pivoted many times during the long series of rejections. The rejections might be telling you that you need to reconsider what you are doing.

I am taking this "why not participating" off your list.

Want to wait until their ideal pitch is ready

Answer: Good enough versus ideal

Many of the entrepreneurs that do a startup come from a science or technical background, and so they are often perfectionists. Thus, in terms of a reason not to participate in a startup pitch competition, they sometimes will tell me that they are waiting until they have just the perfect pitch (ha!), and until then it is not worthwhile to go.

I am betting that if you wait until the ideal pitch is ready, you will be making the pitch from your gravestone. The ideal pitch is a myth. You want to aim for the "good enough" pitch. One that is sound enough that you can make a decent job of representing the startup, and that has considered the aspects that the judges care about (we'll be covering this soon, hang in there).

I am taking this "why not participating" off your list.

Figure it is a waste of time and effort

Answer: How else using time & effort

Some that don't seek to participate in a startup pitch competition will say that it is a waste of time and effort. Let's unpack that bold claim. They might be right, or maybe they might be mistaken.

First, let's consider the time involved. You need to prepare your pitch, which will take time. But, you are likely going to need to have a good pitch in-hand anyway, for use with investors and any other key stakeholders. So, I don't think we should count that as time wasted toward the startup pitch competition. I would counter-argue that it gets you to actually put together a decent pitch and hone it with the competitions, which otherwise it might be much rawer when you are trying to get that $1,000,000 investment.

You need to certainly consider the time required to participate in the event. Most of the competitions are around 2-3 hours in length, sometimes more, sometimes less. That doesn't seem too onerous on your time. There is the time to get there and back. In the olden days, when the competitions were only in say Silicon Beach, it was indeed a time chunk to get there if you didn't already live there. Now, there are competitions all across the country and all around the world. Some are even including now competitors participating remotely.

The effort can be logically viewed in the same manner as the time. I suggest you then need to weigh that against the benefits that we've now earlier listed. I say this because I think you need to consider the ROI on the time and effort invested versus the results and outcomes that can occur. Finally, I would also ask what else the startup is doing that would have an equal return.

I know some that say they would rather focus their energies on pitching strictly to investors and do so when not in a competition or contest. Yes, I get that. If you can do so, and if the other benefits of the startup pitch competition are not of value to you, then I would think it makes sense for you to not participate. But, this is very rare and only a tiny fraction of startups. I am taking this "why not participating" off your list, since I say it is only 1/1000th of a percent that can truly say that not participating is fully justified.

Concerned about the cost to compete

Answer: Costs are usually minimal

Let me say that I well agree that costs for a startup need to be managed very closely. Do not waste any dollars. Usually, the startup is working on fumes. There is though also the danger of the classic penny-wise and pound-foolish. You need to spend wisely. It takes money to make money, as they say. I might have just made a world's record of the most adages in one paragraph.

The costs to participate in the pitch event is usually relatively minor. There is typically a submission fee, with some cases it is free and others that it is maybe $100 or so. By-and-large, most events do not want to lose the chance of having the next Facebook come to pitch simply due to the submission fee.

There is the cost of getting to and from the pitch event. Again, as before, these costs are less these days because you don't necessarily need to fly and get a hotel. If you win a local pitch, it might be a good sign that maybe you should consider going for one of the bigger ones, and thus the travel costs at that juncture might be more justifiable.

There is the cost of your time. This must be balanced against what else you would have used the time for. It must also be balanced against the benefits that we've listed for participating in a startup pitch competition. Overall, I am guessing that most of the time the costs will be minimal and that it should not be a barrier to your participation.

I am taking this "why not participating" off your list.

RECAP OF WHY TO PARTICIPATE

I hope that my above diatribe on the value of participating in a startup pitch competition has opened your eyes and whetted your appetite. You might still have qualms and maybe those are justified.

I would then suggest that you attend as an audience member and see what these competitions are about. Indeed, going as an observer is a less stressful way of easing into it. You can still get some of the benefits that I've listed. Make sure to hobnob. Try to meet the organizers. Explain that you are thinking of participating at a later occasion. They will likely encourage you to do so. Also, don't be surprised if they on-the-spot try to get you to do so at the event, since these events often allow last minute walk-in's to participate.

CHAPTER 2

WHAT HAPPENS AT A STARTUP PITCH COMPETITION

CHAPTER 2

WHAT HAPPENS AT A STARTUP PITCH COMPETITION

PREFACE

There is anxiety about participating in an event that you know nothing about. What will happen? What is expected of you? How should you prepare? These are all great questions to ask. I will try answering these questions in this chapter. I want to make you as comfortable with what will happen as possible, and thus you will then hopefully focus your anxiety not on what mystery lays ahead, but instead focus your energies on how to make the most of the startup pitch competition.

Usually, the winners of the startup pitch competitions have either prepared well or they have attended prior pitch events (or, done both). They tend to have a swagger and confidence that comes across during their pitch. Though, the biggest swagger won't overcome a lousy startup. Furthermore, an excessive swagger can come across as overly brazen and diminish the power of the startup itself. Investors won't want to put money into a startup that has a founder of such arrogance that they won't listen to the investor, and the same is true about the mentors, and even the judges. There is a need to make sure that you have confidence and passion, and yet also display an openness to adjusting and pivoting. Startups are going to need to adjust and pivot, so a founder that seems pigheaded is going to get dinged. They could still possibly win, but it will be harder in comparison to if they weren't quite so closed minded.

CHAPTER 2: WHAT HAPPENS AT A STARTUP PITCH COMPETITION

Startup pitch competitions will vary in terms of some of the details of how they are run. Overall, there is a relatively standard way of how things will proceed. I have prepared a five step chart that helps indicate the normal progression. See Figure 1.

The middle three steps in Figure 1 are what happens at the actual event itself. These three steps are entitled "Check-in & Hobnob," "Pitches & Pitch," and "Feedback & Network," and I will explain each of these steps next.

You should also expect to do the step that precedes the event, the step entitled "Register & Prepare" since it will shape to a great extent how good you do at the startup pitch competition. Likewise, it is prudent to do the post-event step entitled "Follow-up & Adjust," which will help to maximize the value derived from having participated in the startup pitch competition.

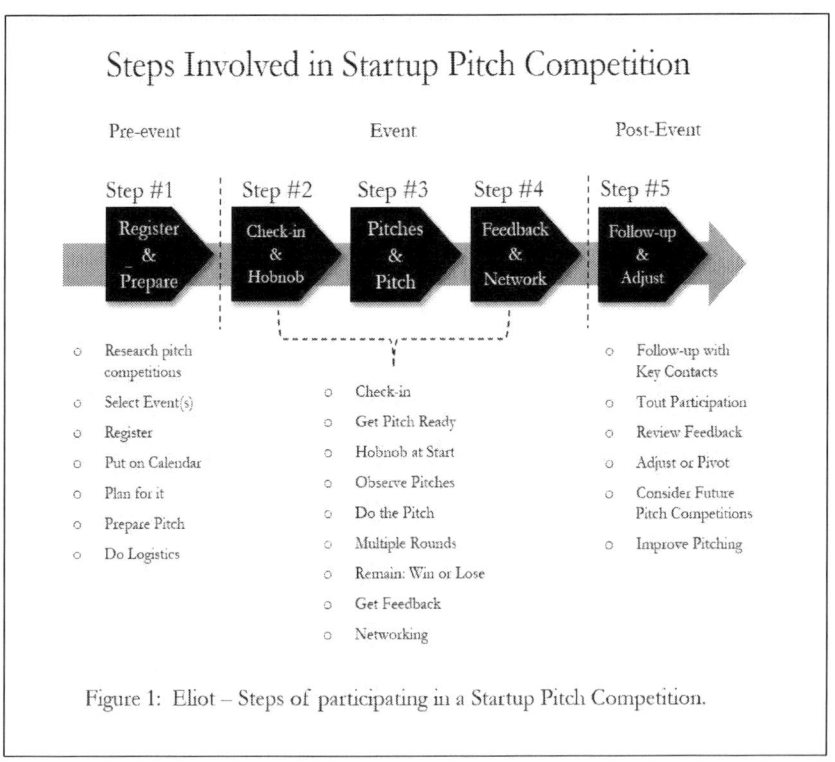

Figure 1: Eliot – Steps of participating in a Startup Pitch Competition.

Step #1: Register & Prepare

Take a look online at various startup pitch competitions in your area. You are likely better off to try one locally, first, and then branch out to other events elsewhere. The travel and logistics costs will be lessened by going with a local event. If there are none locally, or none that you think worth your effort, then by all means certainly look at more distant events.

<u>Registering</u>

Once you find a startup pitch competition that you believe is suitable, make sure to look closely at the registration details and the rules of the pitches. Hopefully, the submission fee is relatively modest. Be watchful for any tacked on special fees that the event organizers try to hook you on. In terms of the rules of the pitches, see if the stated rules look reasonable and fair. Some events will have rules that will tend to make some startups come out better than others. For example, if the pitches are supposed to be for startups that are already funded and ongoing, you will discover that if your startup is earlier and looking for initial seed money that it will probably not win simply because the event is focused on already secured firms. Make sure you are pitching to the right audience as befits your startup status.

Put any key dates on your calendar of aspects that need to be done before you head to the actual event. You might need to provide some kind of added paperwork for the event. You might want to get business cards made, if you don't already have any. You might want to get your prototype ready or any other tangible indication of your product or service. If you pitch only a concept, it will not be as well received as when having something to show or demonstrate.

<u>Preparing</u>

If you are going to demonstrate something during your pitch, please, please, please, rehearse beforehand. I have seen mobile app developers that tried to showcase their app and it bombed out right away. The app got an error and refused to proceed. This was agonizing for the judges, and for the audience, and for the founder. Most attendees want the pitch to go well. They want to see what you have. Going into a pitch without being practiced is just very risky. Of course, we all know that things will go wrong. Murphy's Law that things will go wrong, and go wrong at the worst of times, will already be in play, and so try to diminish the chances by getting yourself fully ready.

Step #2: Check-in & Hobnob

Checking In

Make sure to arrive at the event with plenty of time to spare. We had one participant that came in after the event was already well underway, and breathlessly explained that he had tried to find a place to park, but could not find any available nearby parking. After circling the event location many times, he finally decided to park about a half mile away. He then sprinted to the event. When he came into the event, he was sweating and harried, and worried that because he was late that he would get cut from the event. In this case, he was lucky and he was still allowed to participate. If the event starts at say 6:00 p.m., gauge traffic conditions and the parking situation, and head to the event with sufficient time and contingency time in mind.

Upon arriving at the startup pitch competition, there will usually be a registration desk. You will need to check-in. There might be a badge provided and some last minute instructions and tips indicted. Go look at the area where the pitches will be made. See if there is a stage involved. What about the sound system? If you have something to show like a prototype, what will be the best way to display it? Is there a projection systems so that you can use a PowerPoint presentation?

I remember one event where a founder had brought his startup pitch on his Mac. Turns out the event was not prepared for Apple devices and had hookups for conventional PC's. He had not brought his pitch on a USB memory stick, which they offered to have him put onto a spare PC hooked into the projection system. They decided that he could try emailing it, but they had Wi-Fi connectivity problems and struggled to do so. And on, and on. You get the idea, namely, you will want to arrive early enough to figure out the logistics of how your pitch is going to be undertaken.

Hobnobbing

Once you have done your registration and scoped out the pitch area, it is now time to hobnob. I realize that many founders are so nervous before their presentation that they cannot get themselves to hobnob. If you have brought others of your team or even guests, maybe get them to hobnob for you. Also, there will usually be time to hobnob during breaks and at the end, therefore once your pitch has been done, there is time to do added hobnobbing.

Step #3: Pitches & Pitch

Pitches

During the pitch competition, you will get a chance to see the other pitches. Do not ignore those other pitches! I have seen founders that were preoccupied with mulling over their own pitch and getting mentally ready that they failed to notice the nature of the other pitches.

One time, a startup founder got up to pitch and did not realize that another pitch already given was very similar to her startup. We were all puzzled that she did not bring this up right away. Being in sequence after the first one gave her a chance to do a compare and contrast, but she was oblivious that the other startup had even already pitched.

Make notes about the other pitches. Determine which founders you might want to hobnob with and do some follow-up with them later on.

Watch for what they do right during their pitch, and what they do wrong. If you are adept enough, try to adjust your own pitch based on what seems to be working. I realize it is hard to change your own pitch on-the-fly, and so don't do so if it will more than likely make your pitch worse because it will seem less practiced. At the same time, if you can capitalize on the other pitches, it can be a big boon for your pitch.

Pitch

I recall one pitch that the judges were all seeming to focus on how the founder personally came to the business problem and proposed solution. The judges were wanting to see that the founders had a personal connection to their startup topic, and were not just plucking something out of the air. A founder that I knew, he told me afterward that he had not included in his pitch preparation to explain why he chose the topic that he did. Upon hearing the Q&A with the judges during the other pitches, he realized that it would be helpful to add his personal story. It made a big difference in how well he was received by the judges.

If you ever watch the TV show *Shark Tank*, you can see how impactful a personal story can be. For example, one pitch was about a product inspired by the founder's mother that had died and for which the product could have helped in her last days on earth. Those kinds of stories can be very impactful. An insincere story will do you worse, in that if the story seems contrived it will likely garner backlash. The story should be from the heart. It also should not go on endlessly.

The pitches are usually timed. You will have sometimes 3 minutes, maybe 5 minutes. Some events do a series of rounds. The first round, everyone gets a short amount of time, typically 1 minute or 2 minutes. The first round is shorter because the judges want to weed out startups that aren't ready to really do a true startup pitch. Once they narrow the field to a handful, those handful get a second round of pitching, and a bit more time to pitch.

The pitch time might include Q&A by the judges. This is the part of the pitch that takes you away from your rehearsed canned pitch. This can be the toughest time of the pitch. You need to be able to think on your feet. As always, preparation is the key. The odds are that the questions asked by the judges will be something that you could have predicted would be asked. You can usually include the rest of your team during the Q&A, which can be helpful to you, so that you alone are not only on-the-spot.

Due to the severe time constraints, you won't be able to get your entire startup story told. Things that you leave out will more than likely come up during the Q&A. That's OK, in that as long as you used your canned pitch time wisely, you won't be dinged during Q&A on not having addressed some topics. The judges will realize that you opted to fit in what you could in your speech time.

If you have squandered part of your canned speech time, and thus omitted salient aspects that should have come up, the judges will sometimes ask about those aspects during the Q&A. When they do so, they might also appear upset, since they are likely thinking that you should have covered those topics but misused your canned pitch time. Judges might also be upset with you for other reasons, such as if you seem to cavalier and not taking the pitch seriously, or if you appear distracted and not focused on telling us about your startup, etc.

I recall one pitch that the founder spoke the entire 5 minutes about the business problem. We were all pretty much convinced that he had found a thorny problem that many people face. We had absolutely no idea what his proposed solution was and nor how his startup would enact such a solution. We knew it was a billion dollar market for anyone that could solve the problem. Anyway, immediately when going to Q&A, one of the judges cleared his throat and then with a bit of sarcasm said perhaps the founder might enlighten us about what the actual startup and solution is. This got a sharp laugh from the audience, but at the expense of the founder pitching.

Step #4: Feedback & Network

Feedback

After the pitches are done, there usually will be time to get feedback about your pitch. The judges will retreat to a secluded area to review the pitches, and then come back and announce the winners. During that judging time, you can chat with other participants and see what they say about your pitch and your startup.

Try to find feedback that covers two aspects, namely your pitch as one aspect, and your startup as the other. I mention this due to the notion that you might have a really good pitch, but a lousy business. Or, you might have a lousy pitch, but a great business. You need to discern which is which. Some feedback will come across as though your business is not very sharply defined, but it could be that the pitch did this, and that your business is actually very sharply defined. Likewise, you might get feedback that your pitch was stupendous but the business itself needs a lot of work to make it more sustainable.

Once the winners are announced, there might be a small ceremony for the winners, and then the event "ends" – but this ending is not the time to just dart out the door. Usually, the venue is available for further discussion and many will mingle around.

Network

One important networking element would be to see if you can go meet the judges once the event ends. Trying to meet them beforehand or during the event can be difficult, not only due to their time constraints but also they might feel that they do not want to be unduly biased toward a particular startup and so avoid much contact beforehand.

Once the pitches have concluded and the winners announced, some judges will be more than happy to meet with the participants and provide feedback. In theory, the judges should not reveal the inner deliberations of their fellow judges. Nonetheless, an astute judge can usually consolidate the remarks of their fellow judges and over appropriate feedback.

Some judges are investors and will want to discuss potentially investing in your firm. Some judges are mentors that might want to mentor your firm. Generally, it is well worth trying to hobnob with them. That being said, don't be a pest. Sometimes a founder comes up to a judge and announces in a loud voice that they feel there were cheated by not having won. This kind of reaction will get you feedback, but probably not in the manner befitting being useful.

I realize that if you have not won the competition that you will feel let down. You might not have the energy or vibe to want to talk with the judges. Somehow, find your inner core and get out of that mindset. These judges not only can likely provide helpful feedback, it could make the difference in terms of whether you win at the next pitch you do. Plus, many judges go from one pitch competition to other, and so if you make a positive impression this time that you might find that aiding your next pitch.

Keep in mind that some judges are very busy and will need to dart out the door right away, and so you might not be able to meet them at the end of the competition. In that case, you might consider sending a follow-up email to, and mention that you had hoped to meet them at the end, but realized they had to leave.

Also, keep in mind too that the judges are human. You might approach a judge at the end, and they are really grouchy. Is this because of you? Maybe not. They might not have eaten recently and were hungry the whole time, or maybe they flew to the event and the flight was terrible, or maybe their dog bit them before they came to the event. Try not to overly weigh the reaction of any one judge, since they might be having a bad day and take it out on you.

Step #5: Follow-up & Adjust

<u>Follow-up</u>

It will take time to follow-up, and time is precious, but it could be worthwhile. Connect via LinkedIn with contacts you made (or use other social media). Send emails. Make notes of who you met, and make sure to remember what they said and how you met them. If you just toss the business cards you collected into a drawer of your desk, you will not leverage those contacts. Also, if you don't make notes, you'll likely not ever remember what was discussed.

If you promised to do follow-up, you'd best do so. For example, I know one founder that pitched, lost the event, spoke with a judge, the judge said she was interested in investing, gave a business card to the founder, and asked that the founder follow-up. The founder never did. The judge remembered that the founder did not follow-up, even though the founder had insisted they would. When the two saw each other at a business mixer, the founder tried to apologize, but it was now too late. The judge and investor figured that if the founder was so flaky that they could not do a simple follow-up, trying to do business with them was going to be rough the whole way.

<u>Adjust</u>

Regardless of whether you win or lose the startup pitch competition, the odds are high that you will see something, hear something, meet someone, or otherwise discover an aspect that will spark you to adjust your own ways. This could either be an adjustment of your pitch. Or, it could be a pivot to your business. Be ready and open to doing so.

OTHER THOUGHTS ON WHAT HAPPENS

I have tried to give you a keen sense of what occurs at a startup pitch competition. The format will differ from one event to another. Some will have short pitches, some will have long pitches, some will have only one round, some will have several rounds. Some will even pre-determine who will pitch, by doing a selection process before the event actually occurs.

At some events, they provide tables or booths for the participants, allowing them to showcase their startup. This is sometimes done as part of the normal registration or might cost extra to be able to do. In some cases, the judges are encouraged to go to the booths and see the startups, while in some instances it is a requirement and considered part of the judging process.

Try to find out as much detail about the startup pitch competition beforehand, so that you won't get caught off-guard. Ask the organizers of the event. Check social media to see what others say about the event. Maybe even contact former participants that had been in the event. Though, when doing so, keep in mind that if they did not win, this might cause their viewpoint of the event to be jaded.

YOUR PITCH DECK

The topic of how to put together a pitch deck is well covered online by many web sites, and there are even companies that will prepare your pitch deck for you. I am not going to mention any specific pitch-prep firms here because I don't want to be seemingly endorsing any one over another. Just do a search in your favorite search engine for "startup pitch decks" or "best startup pitches" and you will get a plethora of listings and decks to see, along with online ads for firms that do pitch-decks.

I usually tell founders that want to do-it-yourself that they can just go to Slideshare and do a search there. They will find lots of pitch decks shown in their original manner, including famous ones by big-time companies like AirBnB and others. Take a look at their decks. Essentially go ahead and "copy" the things you like and change the things you don't like, respecting any copyrights, of course.

If you are unfamiliar with what a pitch deck should include, don't worry, because in this book we'll cover the scorecard of the judges, and so you can use the elements of the scorecard as the major points that your pitch deck should include. Try to make your pitch deck visually engaging. Use graphics and do not be overly text or narrative based. Cramming a lot of info on a slide is not usually a good idea, and you will lose your audience and the judges will ding you for it.

I know that it is "politically correct" to bash the idea of using PowerPoint or a similar visual slides package. People bemoan PowerPoints and say how bad they are. I assure you, a well prepared set of slides can outdo someone that is just standing and talking without any visual aids. Hands down. You want the slides to be engaging, simple, and you must be rehearsed and have a talk that coincides with the slides.

Some startup pitch competitions won't allow you to use slides, or they would but they do not have the logistics and equipment for it. Find out beforehand the aspects of a particular event, and even if they say they don't do slides, I'd suggest bringing your deck on a memory stick or on your laptop, just in case you can get a chance to use it.

CHAPTER 3

THE PITCH JUDGES AND HOW THEY THINK

CHAPTER 3

THE PITCH JUDGES AND
HOW THEY THINK

PREFACE

We are going to miniaturize ourselves and sneak into the minds of startup pitch judges. There is a lot going on inside those brains. Some judges will have a very clear and structured mindset about what they are looking for when assessing a startup firm and pitch, while others will have a very cluttered mindset. Judges are human. They have the same foibles as the rest of us. They have biases. They might be having a good day or a bad day when they happen to be serving as a pitch judge.

Whatever might be going on in their heads, the judges should be thinking about what it takes to do a startup. Some pitch competitions use a scorecard to help guide the judges. It is a handy tool. By looking at the scorecard, it reminds the judges what kind of criteria or factors to consider. I have put together a scorecard that pretty much wraps in the other scorecards that I've seen and used. My scorecard has been used at some events and it has gotten positive responses. By showing you the scorecard, I will help guide you toward what you need to do, and thus provide insights about how to win a startup pitch competition. In this chapter, I lay the foundation for the context of a scorecard and what the judges are doing during the pitch competition.

———

CHAPTER 3: THE PITCH JUDGES AND HOW THEY THINK

Let's walk through what the judges will be doing when you are making your pitch at a startup pitch competition. We will go behind-the-scenes to garner what they are considering as judges and how you can then best aim to get their attention and woo them.

In Figure 1, I show a typical layout for a startup pitch competition. On the left side of the diagram, I show that we have a setup, labeled as #1, in which the judges sit behind a long table, they face you as you give your pitch, and the audience is behind you. Meanwhile, there is a moderator lurking around. This setup #1 is pretty common and in a moment I will provide some tips about how to best make your pitch in that situation.

There is another popular layout, which I've labeled as setup #2, and it is shown on the right side of Figure 1. In this layout, you are standing at the front of the area, you are facing the judges and the audience. I realize you might at first glance think that my differentiating the two layouts is kind of silly and maybe nitpicking. I don't think so.

The reason that knowing and using the layout is crucial comes down to this, you are being assessed on two things: (1) Your startup, and (2) Your pitch. If your pitch is messed-up due to the layout and how you use the layout, it can undermine conveying the wonderful nature of your startup.

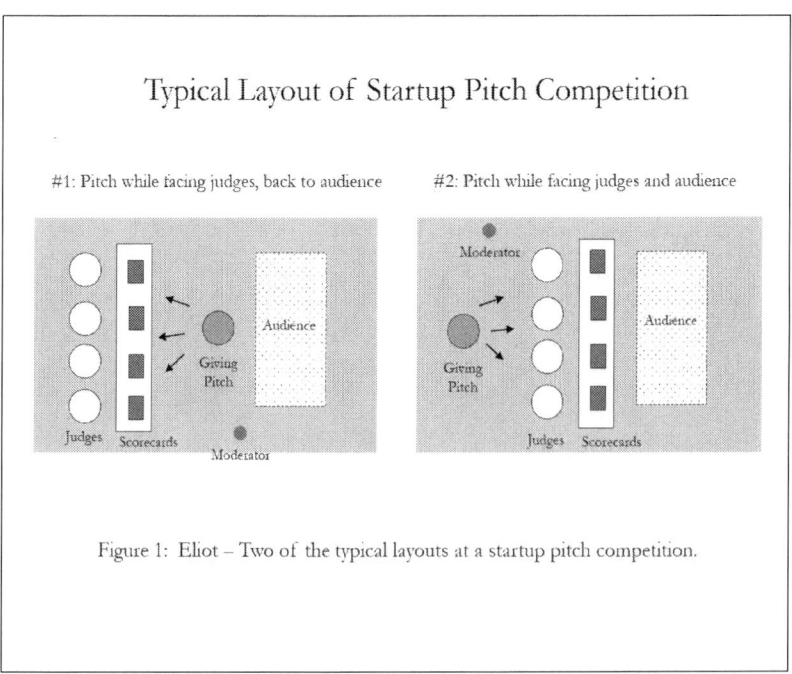

Figure 1: Eliot – Two of the typical layouts at a startup pitch competition.

I see many founders that come to a startup pitch competition and think that their startup is so great that no matter had lousy a job they do when pitching, they will still win the competition because their firm is the next best thing since sliced bread. The problem with this logic is that if the judges cannot figure out that you are making the next best thing since sliced bread, they won't be able to give you high marks on it. Your pitch is the vehicle that conveys what your startup is.

That being said, I have seen some founders that tried very hard to make a good pitch, but were really not very versed in doing so, and they got lucky because the judges ultimately teased out of the founder what was going on with the startup. The Q&A portion can provide an opportunity for a lousy pitch to be resurrected in that the judges can drive the founder toward better articulating what the startup is. The problem here is that you have to then hope that the judges will be astute enough to do so, and that they have the willingness to do so, and that the Q&A time will be sufficient to allow this recovery.

I have seen judges that within the first 30 seconds of a pitch decided that the founder was inept and so then ignored anything else stated. When it got to the Q&A, each judge "passed" in terms of being given a chance to ask questions. No judge asked a single question. Believe it or not, the founder took this as a good sign and I heard him tell a friend as he sat down that "he nailed it" – not realizing that if there aren't any questions it usually is a bad sign. For any startup worth its salt, the odds are that a judge or two will want to know more. They are intrigued and want to dig deeper than the pitch. If nobody is digging, it usually means that they have already decided that there ain't no gold in them hills.

NAVIGATING THE LAYOUT

The setup #1 is a layout that has your back to the audience. I know that we were all taught to not be rude to our audience and make sure to speak to facing your audience. In this case, though, your aim should be the judges. They will determine your fate as to win or lose. You should not try to do the twister speech, whereby you turn back-and-forth trying to somehow face both the judges and the audience at the same time. It is distracting to you, it is distracting to the judges, it is distracting to the audience.

You can sometimes try to move toward the wall, say where I have shown the moderator standing, and try to angle towards both the judges and the audience, but only do this if it makes sense in the context of your pitch and the mood of the room.

In terms of any Audio/Visuals (A/V), some events provide a screen and it will hopefully be in a position that the judges can see it. Try not to face toward the screen and read what your slides indicate, and instead be so rehearsed that you can face the judges and just occasionally glance at the screen.

If there is a microphone, make sure to use it, if it is working properly. I suggest this because many founders think they have a strong voice, and so they object to using the microphone, but then everyone strains to hear what they have to say. Better to use the microphone and be practiced in using one. Of course, if there is no microphone then make sure to speak loudly enough to be well heard. Try not to act like you are yelling at the judges, but that you are just trying to speak clearly and well enough to be readily heard.

Some founders ask me if they should stand in one spot, or whether they should move around. If you are going to pace feverishly then I'd say stand in one spot. If you are able to gracefully move around, and still keep facing the judges, and not be distracted from telling your pitch, I'd say you can move around. Basically, if you aren't a good speaker, you will likely be better to stand in place.

Standing in place does not mean that you should act like you are mummified. One founder kept his arms at his sides the entire time. Some of the judges whispered that maybe he had some kind of motor reflex issues. Turns out he had been advised that he should not wave around his arms and hands, because it would be distracting. If you want to exhibit passion and excitement, you pretty much do need to wave your arms and hands. This does not mean you should be making motions like a college cheerleader. You should have a relatively natural set of motions and use them for effect at the right times of the pitch.

In the second layout that I have labeled #2, you are facing everyone. This is easier on you. It is the traditional kind of setup for doing any kind of public speaking. You might also be up on a stage. Sometimes it is a full stage that could accommodate a Shakespeare play, while other times it is a riser that happens to have a semblance of a stage.

The main trick with this setup #2 is that you should try to look at the judges. In layout #1, I recommended that you look at the judges, and that is pretty much easy to do. In layout #2, you might be tempted to look over the heads of the judges at the rest of the audience. I vote that you try to look at the judges, rather than looking off toward the audience. By looking at the judges, you convey that you are speaking to them. This is better in terms of making a positive impression on the judges. If you seem to be pitching to the audience, the judges will sometimes feel like you have become an orator and are there to do a stage play.

When I suggest that you look at the judges, do not do a stare down with them. Do not try to appear like you are staring directly at them. I have had some founders that almost seemed to be giving the evil eye to one of the judges. It creeped us all out. Instead, your gaze should be toward the judges, sweeping back and forth, slowly, and with purpose. No rapid head movements like you are at a ping pong match.

The moderator will sometimes be very active during your pitch. They might interrupt you, they might instruct you to speak up or be less loud. They might tell you stand over on the side. They might stop you midstream and make an announcement. One never knows. The key is that don't let it rattle you. Take the instruction, try to comply, and then continue with the pitch.

Be aware that some moderators will do a quick introduction of you, and then hand things over to you. For the next 3 minutes or whatever the pitch time is, the moderator won't interfere, even if there is a fire in the room and an atom bomb hits. These kinds of moderators believe that it is your pitch time and by gosh nothing should disrupt it. I mention this because some founders look constantly at the moderator, waiting for instructions, and it becomes kind of an odd circumstance, wherein the founder looks over at the moderator, so we judges look at the moderator. The moderator takes no action. We look back at the founder. Repeat this. It is very distracting.

We will next discuss the set of pitching participants. Take a look at Figure 2.

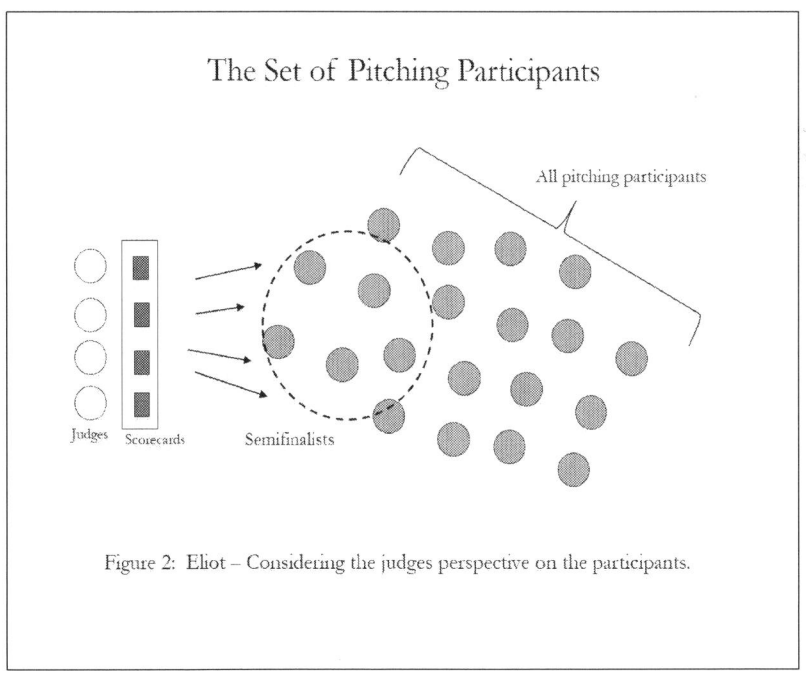

Figure 2: Eliot – Considering the judges perspective on the participants.

YOU ARE NOT ALONE

At times, it is easy to forget that you are not the only person making a pitch at these competitions. You are thinking about you. You care how you are doing and how your pitch went. That makes sense. From the judging perspective, keep in mind that we are seeing a whole bunch of these pitches. One after another. It can become mind numbing.

There is also another fatigue factor for the judges, namely that after a while the startups seem to blur together. I realize from your perspective that you believe your story and startup is unique. For the judges, they are hearing one pitch, another pitch, and they at times the pitches seem to be the same overall. Yes, the nature of the business itself might differ, but it becomes hard to remember which one was which.

Usually, there is some mechanism for the judges to filter out the total set or population of participants and narrow the field to semifinalists. Obviously, your goal would be to make the semifinals. If you aren't in the semifinals then you aren't going to win the competition.

This brings up an important point, which might at first glance seem obvious, but often participants at a startup pitch competition seem to somehow not know it or not take it into account:

At a startup pitch competition, you just need to win over the other participants, which does not necessarily make you the absolute best in the world, but just the "best" at that event on that occasion.

The point is that by watching the other participants give their pitches, you hopefully will see things that help guide any adjustments for your pitch. You are trying to adjust your pitch to fit to the circumstances of that particular moment. You need to standout in comparison to the other pitches taking place.

I have had founders that were hesitant to participate because they did not think of themselves or their startup as "the best" and so talked themselves out of participating. I pointed out that they needed to be not an absolute best in comparison to all startups since the time of the Greeks and Romans, but just had to be the "best" at the specific event. If you are competing against startups that all look like yours, try to find something unique that you can harp on. It might not have been what you had in mind when you showed up, but it can make the difference in terms of being memorable and standing apart from the pack.

THE JUDGING DELIBERATION

At some point, the judges are usually told to get together and assess what they have seen and heard. The judges might do this multiple times, doing for each round, if there are multiple rounds involved. Sometimes, the judges do this deliberation where they have been seated all along. They quietly try to compare notes and chat among themselves. I often find this to be somewhat awkward, because the founders making the pitches or the audience members can perhaps overhear the discussions. Though they might want to overhear, it is rough as a judge to discuss openly and with criticism the pitches and startups when being overheard.

Many events will ask the judges to go to a private room that has been set aside for the judging deliberations. As shown in Figure 3, the judges typically sit around a large conference table, have their notes and water bottles and coffee in front of them, and engage in a spirited dialogue.

I say spirited dialogue because it usually is just that. Judges will argue vehemently in favor of this pitch or that one. Judges will declare that a particular pitch or startup should not win, and should never ever win. Other judges will see things the opposite and argue that a particular pitch or startup must win or the earth will stop spinning. Passions often run high.

Typical Layout of Judges Deliberation

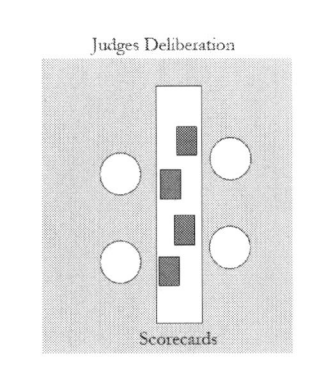

Figure 3: Eliot – Typical layout for judges deliberation.

Ultimately, in a process that is often nebulous and left to the discretion of the judges, a decision will be reached by the judges. It might involve a vote. It might involve just head nods. It might be formalized with having to write things down, or it might be informal. The event might have specific guidelines for the judges. Or, it might believe that the judges can decide among themselves how they want to make the selections.

Given that the deliberation process is crucial to your fate, what can you do to increase your odds of rising to the top during the deliberations? The answer relates to the scorecards.

THE IMPORTANCE OF SCORECARDS

You might have noticed that in Figure 1, Figure 2, and Figure 3, I had shown that there are scorecards near the judges. Some events have a formal scorecard that is handed to the judges and they are supposed to appropriately fill-in for each pitch. Other times an event will just encourage the judges to take notes, essentially creating their own informal scorecard.

The scorecard is an important element for the judges and for you. For the judges, it helps them remember what they saw and heard. They will be able to use the scorecard during the judging deliberations.

Without a scorecard or the equivalent, they will be relying just on fading and vague memories. Usually in that circumstance, whichever judge seems to have the most command of what happened and what the pitches were, will often drive the discussion of the judges. They have the facts, while the others are struggling to remember the facts.

You might be puzzled that the judges could not remember each pitch with full clarity. Well, suppose there are pitches that are being made for 3 minutes each. Suppose the field of pitches is twenty participants. Let's assume that there is a two minute Q&A for each pitch. Let's assume that there is a time gap of about 1-2 minutes between each pitch, giving time for the pitch just made to sit down and the next pitch to come up and get started.

Add up the time. It could be around 1 ½ to two hours. Finally, imagine that after two hours of being bombarded by pitch after pitch, the judges go into a room. They need to remember each pitch. The pitches that don't standout are going to be the least likely to be remembered and least likely to be discussed.

Indeed, the field is usually quickly culled by the judges. Rather than going through each one, they often short cut to ask which ones seemed to rise up, and then focus on discussing those. Again, this is on a relative basis.

Of the twenty that we are pretending took place, and if the first deliberation round is about cutting to the top five, the judges will usually instantly knock out ten, and focus on the remaining ten to get it narrowed to the top five.

If you knew what the scorecard is, you could try to make sure that you hit the key points of it. In this manner, at least during the deliberations the judges cannot say that well, we didn't hear this or that about that particular startup. Also, you can make sure you have covered your bases, especially since during the Q&A you might look weak if you cannot answer a fundamental question about your startup.

Again, a scorecard can help you on preparing. The odds are that the event itself won't let you see the scorecard template (some do, but it is rare). In the next chapter, we will take a close look at a scorecard template and use it to get you ready and increase your odds of prevailing at the startup pitch competition.

BOOTHS OR TABLES

I earlier mentioned that some startup pitch competitions will have booths or tables for each startup. Usually, the booths or tables are to be used prior to the pitches themselves taking place, and might also be available after the pitches for attendees that want to go over to the booth or table to talk with a particular startup that caught their eye during the pitches.

If you are able to have a booth or table, make sure to treat it seriously. I say this because I have seen some founders and their team that had a booth or table and did little to present their startup in any favorable manner. The booth or table was not adorned with anything about the startup, and they just stood there, waiting for attendees to ask them about their startup. This is likely to undermine you, your startup, and your pitch.

Often, the judges come to look at the firms before the pitches, going up to the respective booths and tables. Sometimes the judges will announce who they are, while other times the judge is just quietly kicking the tires. You need to therefore treat every person that comes to your booth or table with the proper respect and attention. You never know who they might be. Maybe a big investor, maybe a great contact to investors, maybe a judge at the competition, etc.

That being said, don't let one person monopolize your attention. I have stood behind some long-talker that monopolized a founder and I never got a chance to find out what the startup did. Make sure you and whomever is "manning" your booth or table knows how to talk about the startup, they need to know how to interact with people, they need to know how to use the time effectively and how to deal with the monopolizing individuals and others that will likely come to the booth or table.

If possible, adorn your space with signage that befits your startup. You should have something that is readily visible that indicates your firm name, your problem/solution, and your product/service. Having a sharp looking logo helps. Having a prototype is great. Doing a demonstration is great, but only if the demo can be done relatively quickly, and occur nearly error free. Also, think carefully about how to do the demo. I saw a dentist that had a new device to freeze the inside of your mouth, and at first they were asking attendees to open their mouths to feel the freezing effect. Probably a lawsuit was waiting in the wings on that one.

Having a handout is good too. You should have business cards, which is one kind of handout. Another handout is a flyer or some other object or item to provide to those that stop at the booth. I say this with the realization that providing handouts might start to cost you some dough. Try to have a relatively inexpensive handout that you can give to the masses, and then have something else a bit nicer that once you have "qualified" an attendee that you might give it to that person, assuming they are a higher worthy contact.

Speaking of qualifying attendees, if the event allows you to do so, try to collect business cards or contact info from the attendees that stop at your booth or table. One of the easiest ways to connect with someone would be to use social media such as LinkedIn. Your startup should have a LinkedIn page, along with potentially being present in other social media too.

For the booth or table, you'll want to find out beforehand what the size is, what signage is permitted, the time that they allow to start setup, the time that they expect you to dismantle your booth or table, and other logistics. When doing something at the booth that requires electricity, such as running a laptop or large-size monitor, find out beforehand if electrical power will be available. If so, probably wise to bring along some extension cords and power strips. Be prepared that if they don't have power available, what else will you do? For example, maybe create a poster board as a back-up, and so if you cannot show someone on your laptop then at least you can use the poster board.

Having a booth or table is both a blessing and a curse. It can take a lot of extra work to handle, add to your preparations, and distract you from the actual pitch (because you were dealing with that darned booth!). On the other hand, it can gain interest that whets the appetite of judges and attendees for the pitch, and can provide a safe harbor after the pitch whereby attendees can come over to offer feedback or assistance to your startup. Do not underestimate the work required and plan accordingly.

CHAPTER 4

USE THE LBE SCORECARD
AS YOUR GUIDE

CHAPTER 4

USE THE LBE SCORECARD
AS YOUR GUIDE

PREFACE

A scorecard is an essential tool for judges. It allows them to keep track of each pitch. They can score each pitch based on various factors or criteria. During a startup pitch competition, there are lots of pitches to be seen. When the judges deliberate, they often rely upon their notes and a scorecard to discuss the merits of each pitch and the respective startup. Using the scorecard can spark healthy debates among the judges about why each judge scored in a particular way.

The scorecard forces the judges to go beyond just pure emotion and be more factual about what they have seen and heard. If a judge believes that a particular startup and pitch was the best, they would need to explain how they arrived at a scoring that reflects that opinion. If they believe that a particular pitch and startup was not the best, they would need to show the scoring that indicates that aspect.

For you, the point is that by knowing what is usually included on a scorecard, you can prepare your pitch and make sure that your startup will score well. This also has the larger capability of making you think carefully about your startup and perhaps even reveal weaknesses to you that you might otherwise have not considered.

———

CHAPTER 4: USE THE LBE SCORECARD AS YOUR GUIDE

There are lots of different scorecards used in startup pitch competitions. Some scorecards have just a few factors or criteria. Some have a more extensive list. Some require a scoring on a scale of 1 to 5, while others are 1 to 10. There are even scorecards that have no numeric scoring and instead simply provide note-taking space for the judges to make notes.

I have used a wide variety of these scorecards. Let's boil them down into their essence. The essence consists of the business elements that a startup needs to consider and have a strategy and capability in. Take a look at Figure 1. I will explain each of the boxes shown on the diagram.

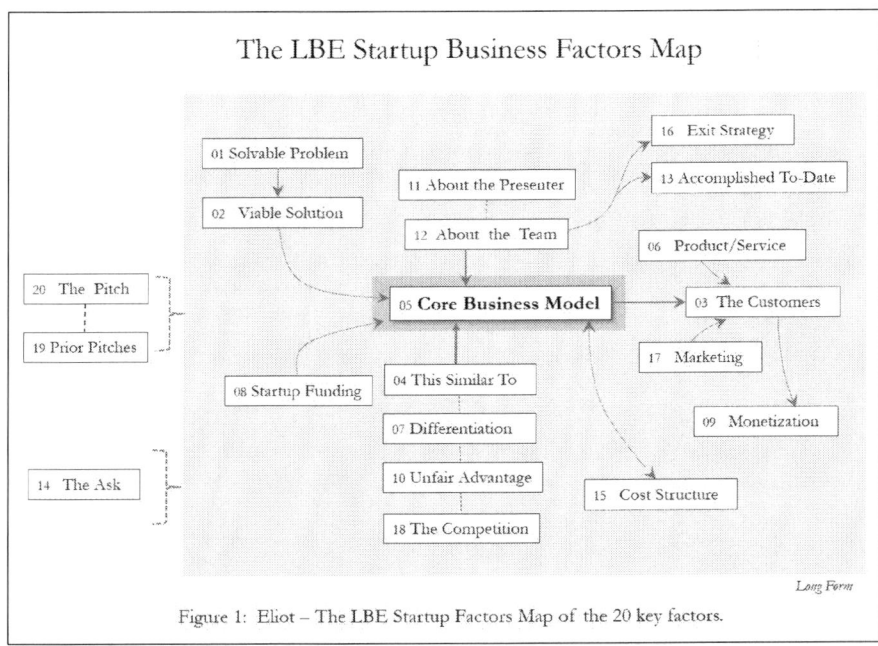

Figure 1: Eliot – The LBE Startup Factors Map of the 20 key factors.

Let's walk through the diagram. Think about your own startup as I do so. First, note that there is a shaded area. In the upper left of the shaded area, I have listed "Solvable Problem" and "Viable Solution" (they are numbered, whereby Solvable Problem is listed as "01" and the Viable Solution is listed as "02").

On the next page, I provide the Figure 1 shown horizontally so that it might be easier for you to read it.

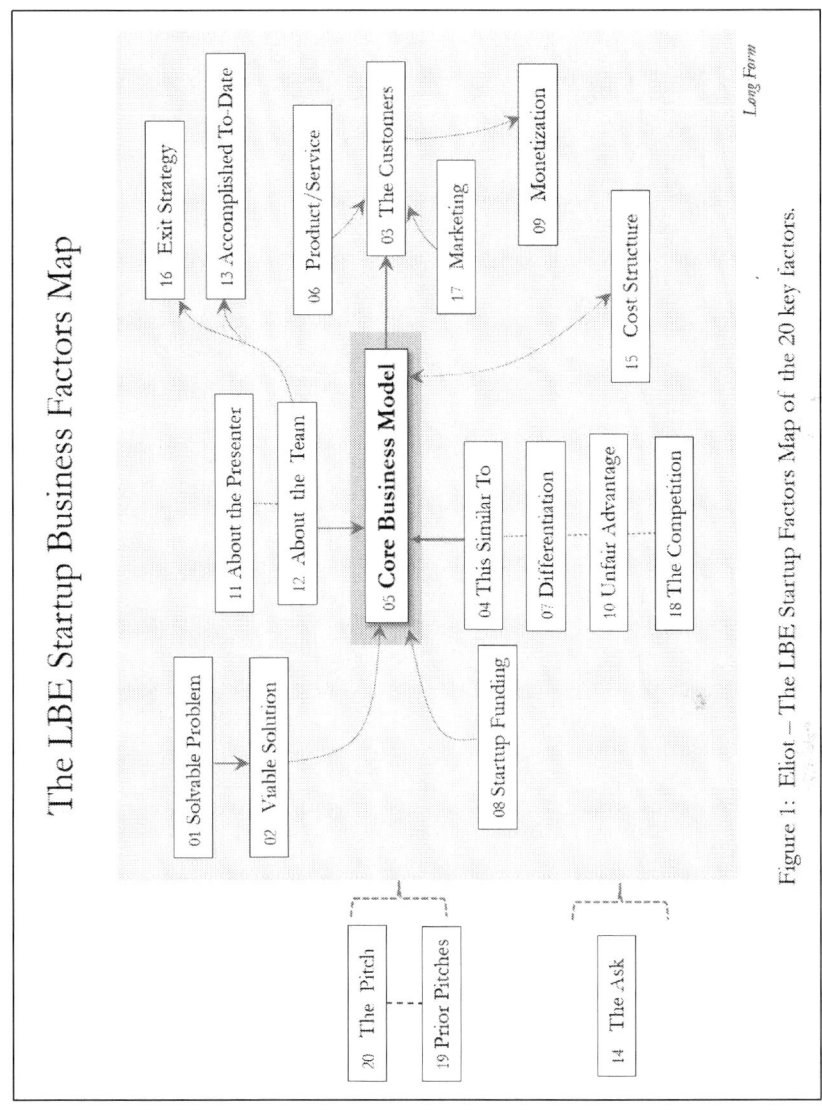

Figure 1: Eliot — The LBE Startup Factors Map of the 20 key factors.

Your startup needs to have a clearly identified Problem that it is trying to solve. I phrase this as a "solvable" problem because it won't do much good if you come up with a problem for which no solution is possible. How can you propose a business that does something to solve the problem if the problem itself is not solvable? Keep that in mind.

Judges are eager to know what the problem is that you are going to be solving. If the first thing you do is identify an unsolvable problem, you have already dug a hole that you won't be able to get out of. The odds are that your claimed solution will not fit to the stated problem, and you will be accused of solving some other kind of problem. Your problem and your solution must match.

Notice that I said that you need to have a "viable" solution. This is not by accident. If you have a solution that is not viable, your business won't go anywhere. You need to have both a "Solvable Problem" and a "Viable Solution" in order to be considered a startup that will have a reasonable chance at succeeding.

Next, assuming that you have a solvable problem that you can describe, and a viable solution that you can describe, your next element is to indicate what Core Business Model you are pursuing. This Business Model needs to fit to the solvable problem and the viable solution. If you have a Business Model that does not fit, you will get dinged that your model is not going to achieve the solving of the problem.

Notice that I say "Core" in terms of your Business Model. Your model can be very extensive and have lots of components. In your pitch, you won't have much time to get into all the details. The crux of your Business Model is the "core" part and that's what you need to be able to describe.

A QUICK WALK THROUGH

Later in this book, I will provide further details on each of the elements shown on Figure 1.

Let's do a fast walk through of the rest of the Figure 1 diagram.

Your "Core Business Model" should link to your "The Customers" in terms of those that would be making use of your products or services ("Product/Service" is shown just above the "The Customers" box). There is "Marketing" that feeds into "The Customers" because you need to have some means to ensure that your customers know of the products or services that you are offering.

Somehow your firm will need to produce revenue, which is described in today's parlance as achieving "Monetization" (which is shown just below the "Customers" box). There will be costs associated with your firm and its aim of providing a product or service to customers, so the box "Cost Structure" is shown below the "Core Business Model" box. Your startup will need funding, which is shown as a "Startup Funding" box that leads into your "Core Business Model" box.

Look underneath the "Core Business Model" box. You will see that there is a box that says "This Similar To" which refers to the notion that judges will right away want to figure out how your startup is similar to other kinds of businesses. It is almost like a movie. When you tell someone that you just saw a movie, they will usually want to know what it is similar to. Was the movie like some other action film or romantic movie? It helps them to quickly get a sense of where the movie fits. The same happens with a startup.

Your startup should in some fashion differentiate itself from other like businesses ("Differentiation" box). You should also have an "Unfair Advantage" in that your firm creates a barrier to entry or leverages such a barrier to prevent competitors or at least make it hard for your competition. This brings up that you need to be able to articulate "The Competition" that you see yourself going against.

Above the "Core Business Model" box, I have listed that the judges will be assessing the presenter "About the Presenter" and also will be assessing the team that has been assembled for the startup ("About the Team"). Judges want to know what the exit strategy of the startup might be, and so to upper right side of the shaded area you will see the "Exit Strategy" box. The judges also want to know what your startup has accomplished to-date, "Accomplished To-Date" which might be that it has not yet done much, or might be that it is already well along the way on its efforts.

Outside of the shaded area, on the left side of the diagram, there are some additional boxes. One box is "The Pitch" which means that the judges are assessing the pitch that was given. The judges also will want to know if you have already done pitches, and so the "Prior Pitches" box is shown. Finally, and the element that often is omitted by founders during their pitches is "The Ask" – this is crucial for your pitch, since it establishes what you want from others to help make your startup progress.

I realize that it seems like a lot of boxes on the diagram. When you think about it carefully, you will realize that all of the boxes serve a useful purpose. Suppose we omitted a box. Let's pretend we took the box "Cost Structure" off the diagram. This implies that you have no idea about what costs your business will incur. A business that has no idea of the costs will bleed money. Eventually, the business will fail. A business needs to make money to keep going. We have seen a lot of high-tech startups that manage to go many years without making a profit, and that is feasible, but for most startups you need to at least know what kinds of costs you will have. Furthermore, when asked what kind of funding you need, you cannot answer that question fully without a sense of the costs you face.

Let's now take the Figure 1 diagram and make it into a scorecard. Take a look at Figure 2. You can see the same elements that were on the diagram.

The numbering of the elements is more for reference purposes than due to priority. We could argue endlessly about which of these twenty elements is more important than the other. I would assert that they are all valuable in their own right, and that when looked at in totality is reflects aptly what a startup needs to address.

Judge name:	**Official LBE Scorecard for Startup Pitch Competitions**	Instructions: Make copies of this form, use one per pitch, each judge separately scores.	Date:	Reference #:

Startup Business Name: | Pitch Presented by:

These can be addressed in any order. 1 2 3 4 5 Score	These can be addressed in any order. 1 2 3 4 5 Score	Brief Notes
01 The Solvable Problem: ○○○○○ Is it real, an issue or need or pain, scoped, sizable?	11 About the Presenter: ○○○○○ Background, expertise, personal drivers?	
02 The Viable Solution: ○○○○○ Solves stated problem, viable, practical?	12 About the Team: ○○○○○ Who is involved, relevance, commitment?	
03 The Customers: ○○○○○ Target market, reachable, right for this solution?	13 Accomplished To-Date: ○○○○○ Concept or formed up, MVP as yet, latest status	
04 This is Similar To: ○○○○○ How compares & contrasts to prior solutions?	14 The Ask: ○○○○○ What do you want, basis for the pitch, the ask?	
05 Core Business Model: ○○○○○ Stated model befitting the Viable Solution?	15 Cost Structure: ○○○○○ Understand costs, scalability?	
06 Product/Service: ○○○○○ Defined product and/or services befitting Model?	16 Exit Strategy: ○○○○○ What is your end game, the ideal exit(s)?	
07 Differentiation ○○○○○ How is this a Unique Value Proposition (UVP)?	17 Marketing: ○○○○○ How promote, price, channels, market this?	
08 Startup Funding: ○○○○○ Bootstrap, FFF, Angel, Crowd, Incubator, VC, mix	18 Competitors: ○○○○○ Who is competition, their weaknesses or gaps?	
09 Monetization: ○○○○○ Sources of revenue, ongoing stream, runway	19 Prior Pitches: ○○○○○ Done prior pitches, if so win or lose, any pivoting?	Total Score (max 100)
10 Unfair Advantage: ○○○○○ Is there IP, barriers to entry, potential threats?	20 The Pitch ○○○○○ Engaging, used time well, conveyed aptly?	Give 0 for any score if item not addressed

Copyright © Dr. Lance B. Eliot. All Rights Reserved.　Long Form

For each element, the judge would score the startup on a scale of 1 to 5, with the score of 1 being low and the score of 5 being high. If a pitch fails to address an element, the judge would put a score of zero, since they otherwise have no indication of what the startup has done or plans to do on that element (sometimes judges will make guesses based on what else they have heard during the pitch).

The score is marked on the bubbles next to each element. The score is also placed into the box that is under the heading of "Score" and this makes it easier to tally the points. Once the pitch is completed, the judge adds up the scores and puts that into the box in the lower right side that says "Total Score" (which at 5 points per element can be at most a score of 100, that's 5 points times 20 elements equals 100 points).

On the next page, I show the same scorecard horizontally.

L B E — **Official LBE Scorecard for Startup Pitch Competitions**

Judge name: Instructions: Make copies of this form, use one per pitch, each judge separately scores.   Date: Reference #:

Startup Business Name: Pitch Presented by:

These can be addressed in any order.   1 (Low) 2 3 4 5 (High)   Score

01	The Solvable Problem:	Is it real, an issue or need or pain, scoped, sizable?
02	The Viable Solution:	Solves stated problem, viable, practical?
03	The Customers:	Target market, reachable, right for this solution?
04	This is Similar To:	How compares & contrasts to prior solutions?
05	Core Business Model:	Stated model befitting the Viable Solution?
06	Product/Service:	Defined product and/or services befitting Model?
07	Differentiation	How is this a Unique Value Proposition (UVP)?
08	Startup Funding:	Bootstrap, FFF, Angel, Crowd, Incubator, VC, mix
09	Monetization:	Sources of revenue, ongoing stream, runway
10	Unfair Advantage:	Is there IP, barriers to entry, potential threats?

These can be addressed in any order.   1 (Low) 2 3 4 5 (High)   Score

11	About the Presenter:	Background, expertise, personal drivers?
12	About the Team:	Who is involved, relevance, commitment?
13	Accomplished To-Date:	Concept or formed-up, MVP as yet, latest status
14	The Ask:	What do you want, basis for the pitch, the ask?
15	Cost Structure:	Understand costs, scalability?
16	Exit Strategy:	What is your end game, the ideal exit(s) ?
17	Marketing:	How promote, price, channels, market this?
18	Competitors:	Who is competition, their weaknesses or gaps?
19	Prior Pitches:	Done prior pitches, if so win or lose, any pivoting?
20	The Pitch	Engaging, used time well, conveyed aptly?

Brief Notes

Total Score
(max 100)
Give 0 for any score if item not addressed.

Long form

At the top of the form, the judge enters their name, the date, the startup business name, and the names of those that presented the pitch. The judge can also write notes on the scorecard.

For some judges, they might think that scoring twenty elements is excessive. The reality is that the judges will ultimately be thinking about each of these elements, whether they realize it or not. Scoring each element is often done quickly and in association with other of the elements. When the pitch starts and describes usually the problem, solution, and core business model, those three elements can be all scored at the same moment.

SHORT FORM SCORECARD

Some scorecards do not have this full set of elements, and assumes that the judges will know or think about all of these elements. I below indicate the key elements that many other scorecards only show. The highlighted six elements are often perceived as essential for any pitch. The others are considered by some to be "nice to mention" but are otherwise assumed to exist.

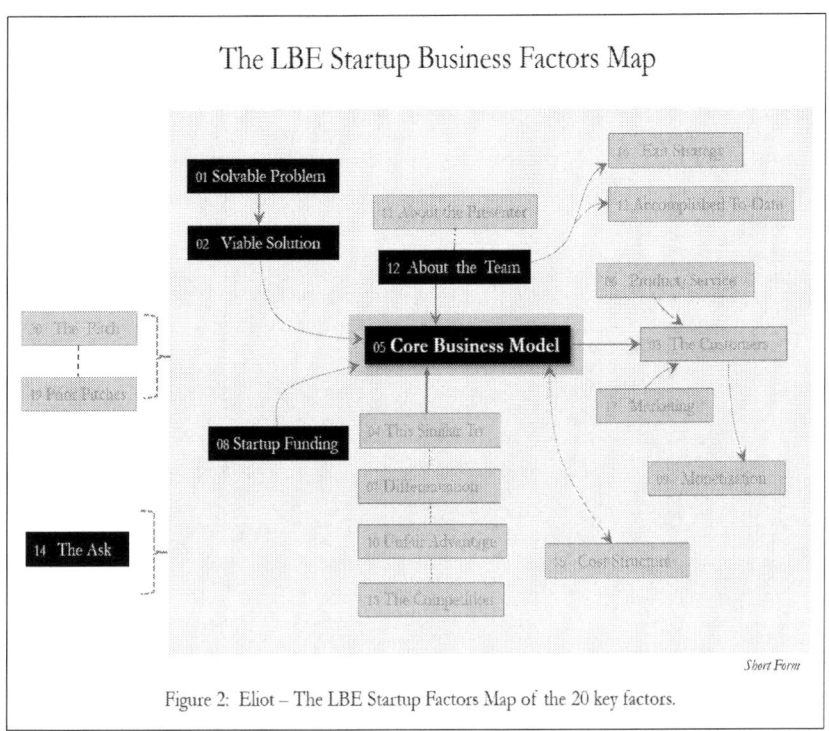

Figure 2: Eliot – The LBE Startup Factors Map of the 20 key factors.

So, the short version of the scorecard form concentrates on these six elements:

01: Solvable Problem

02: Viable Solution

05: Core Business Model

12: About the Team

08: Startup Funding

14: The Ask

For judges, if they know the problem, solution, core business model, the team involved, the startup funding, and what you are asking for, they often believe it is sufficient to get an overall sense of the status and nature of your startup.

Here is the short form version:

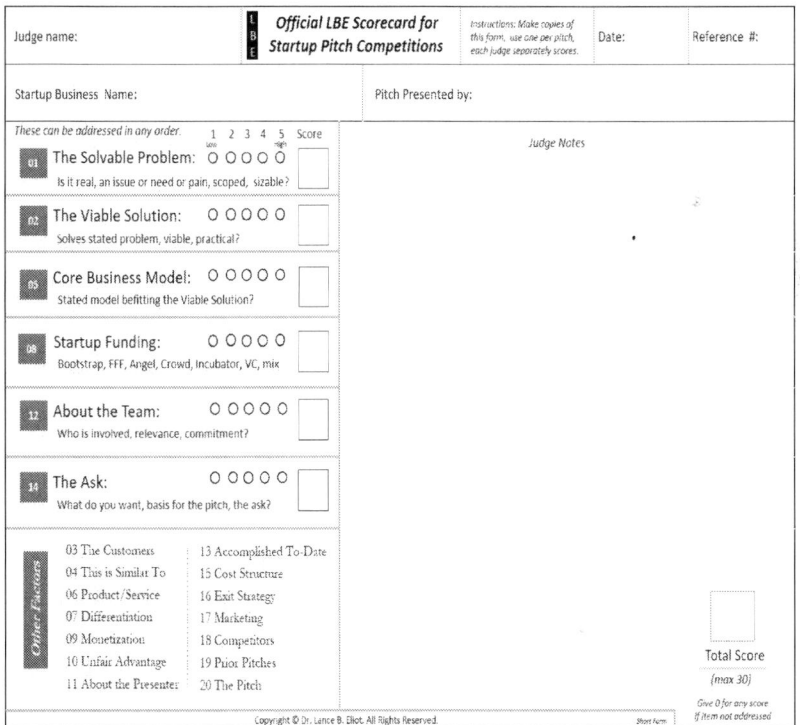

It is shown horizontally on the next page so that you can more easily see it.

L B E Official LBE Scorecard for Startup Pitch Competitions

Judge name:

Instructions: Make copies of this form, use one per pitch, each judge separately scores.

Date:

Reference #:

Startup Business Name:

Pitch Presented by:

These can be addressed in any order.

		1 Low	2	3	4	5 High	Score
01	The Solvable Problem: Is it real, an issue or need or pain, scoped, sizable?	O	O	O	O	O	
02	The Viable Solution: Solves stated problem, viable, practical?	O	O	O	O	O	
05	Core Business Model: Stated model befitting the Viable Solution?	O	O	O	O	O	
08	Startup Funding: Bootstrap, FFF, Angel, Crowd, Incubator, VC, mix	O	O	O	O	O	
12	About the Team: Who is involved, relevance, commitment?	O	O	O	O	O	
14	The Ask: What do you want, basis for the pitch, the ask?	O	O	O	O	O	

Other Factors

- 03 The Customers
- 04 This is Similar To
- 06 Product/Service
- 07 Differentiation
- 09 Monetization
- 10 Unfair Advantage
- 11 About the Presenter
- 13 Accomplished To-Date
- 15 Cost Structure
- 16 Exit Strategy
- 17 Marketing
- 18 Competitors
- 19 Prior Pitches
- 20 The Pitch

Judge Notes

short form

Total Score
_____
(max 30)

Give 0 for any score if item not addressed

WHAT JUDGES THINK

So, what do judges think about when assessing your startup and your pitch? You now have an answer to that question.

Specifically, the judges want to know:

- ✓ What is your stated problem?
- ✓ What is your stated solution?
- ✓ What is your core business model?
- ✓ What are your products or services?
- ✓ Who are your customers?
- ✓ What is your startup most similar to?
- ✓ What funding has your startup received?
- ✓ What is your cost structure?
- ✓ How will you market your products/services?
- ✓ How will you monetize the firm?
- ✓ What differentiates your startup?
- ✓ What is your unfair advantage over others?
- ✓ Who is your competition?
- ✓ Who is on your team?
- ✓ What is your exit strategy?
- ✓ What have you accomplished to-date?
- ✓ Who is the presenter?
- ✓ What other pitches have you done?
- ✓ What is your Ask?

And, they will also assess your Pitch.

They will then be comparing your startup and your pitch to the other startups and pitches that are undertaken at the startup pitch competition, based on those elements. How big and important is your stated problem? Is your solution viable and is it unique and defensible from competition? Do you have the proper team assembled to be able to pull off this startup? And so on, they will use these elements to gauge how good your startup is.

HOW BIG CAN YOU GO

One aspect that is especially crucial during your pitch is the size potential of your market and the chances of your firm grabbing a hefty chunk of that market. This is something you need to get immediately in your pitch, in the sense that you want to at the start of the pitch make sure to impress the judges as to the size and potential that exists for your startup.

Why is that important? Well, imagine that you are going to transform the market for left-handed Eskimos that are frozen food fanatics. You have identified a solvable problem which is that they are not able to open existing frozen food packages due to those packages being made to accommodate right-handed Eskimos, and your viable solution is a new patent-pending left-hand opening frozen food package for Eskimos. It is exciting that you have a solvable problem and a viable solution.

It is not though very exciting as to the size of the market. How many Eskimos are there? How many of those are left-handed? How many of those are frozen food fanatics? That is the total market size you are aiming at. I dare say it will be pretty small. You don't even need to have exact numbers, just approximations are good enough. The point is whether you have found a market that is bigger than a bread box or smaller than a bread box. Generally, investors want the bigger than a bread box market sizes.

The reason for the need of a bigger market is to have a chance at big revenue numbers and hopefully then big profits. Take a look at Venture Capital (VC) firms and you'll see that they pretty much bet on startups that are swinging at the fences, aiming at really gigantic markets. The VC's realize that for them to make a hefty return on investing in your firm, there has got to be big revenue numbers down the pike.

Suppose a VC puts $3 million into your business for 10% of the shares. The typical VC ultimately wants maybe 10x (ten times) to 20x (twenty times) their investment when they eventually cash out. That means that they would need to get $30-$60 million when they cash out. They only have 10% of your firm, so you would need to have a market cap (total market value which is your per share price times the number of shares, essentially, simplified) of like $300 million. You are probably only to get there with a revenue potential in the many hundreds of millions of dollars in a market that is probably a billion or billions in dollars in size.

Angel investors usually aim to put maybe $50,000 to $150,000 into your firm, and so they are often more amenable to smaller market sizes. But if you ultimately want to get the big guns to possibly invest, you need to be positioning into a big enough market. Many times I have had to prod a founder during the Q&A portion of the pitch to tell us the market size. If you don't know it, you'd better figure it out real quick, since a blank stare to that question is a losing proposition.

CHAPTER 5

SELF-DIAGNOSING YOUR STARTUP VIA LBE SCORECARD

CHAPTER 5

SELF-DIAGNOSING YOUR STARTUP
VIA LBE SCORECARD

PREFACE

Now that we have taken a look at the scorecard, let's next have you do a self-diagnosis of your startup and your pitch by using the scorecard. This will allow you to gauge how well you are doing as a startup, and also gauge how well you might score during a startup pitch competition.

For this self-diagnosis, you as the founder should seriously and with thoughtful reflection score your startup using the elements of the scorecard. This can be painful. Some founders refuse to think about how their startup is doing. They harbor a dream and do not want to pop the dream. I assure you that if you won't pop the dream, the judges will do so. You are better off to have first figured out what you are doing well and where you are doing poorly, and either be ready to explain why you are doing poorly on some elements or shore them up before you make your pitch.

As part of the self-diagnosis, I also recommend that you use a mentor to fill-in the scorecard too. Your mentor will hopefully bring a less biased view than your own viewpoint, in the sense that the mentor can look at you from the "outside" and provide a more probing assessment. Not all mentors can or are willing to do so, but you should urge your mentor to try and do so, since being blunt will do you more good than hiding and having you get dinged during the competition.

CHAPTER 5: SELF-DIAGNOSING YOUR STARTUP VIA LBE SCORECARD

The scorecard covered in the prior chapter can be an extremely valuable tool for you and your startup. You should be able to have a cogent strategy and approach for each of the elements. If you are not able to well articulate your approach for any of the elements, it means you have not covered all your bases. Each element not only is important on its own, but they are also integrated together in that the whole mesh can come apart if one piece fails. It is the classic "the weakest link in the chain" notion, which, if that link breaks it could jeopardize everything else.

Some advisers and mentors are eager to find that weak link and help you to shore it up. It is what they do. They help look at the big picture, while you as a founder are usually focused on just a few of the elements. By the way, I am not saying that you need to be an expert in each of the elements, and in fact you will likely need help from others to figure out many of the elements, but as the founder you should at least be aware of and familiar with what your startup is doing or intends to do in each of the elements.

I highly recommend you use the scorecard to do a self-diagnosis. Sit down, in a quiet space, and sincerely fill-in the scorecard. Give yourself a realistic score on each element, and make notes. This is your heart-to-heart with yourself. Take a look at the top part of Figure 1.

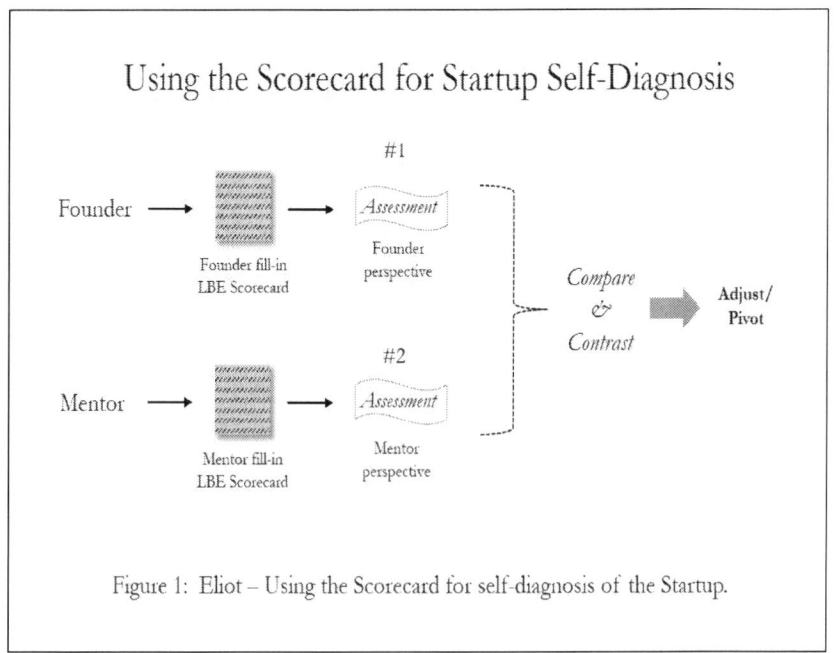

Using the Scorecard for Startup Self-Diagnosis

Figure 1: Eliot – Using the Scorecard for self-diagnosis of the Startup.

So, as shown in Figure 1, you as the founder should fill-in the scorecard and see how you scored. Now, I realize it will be difficult to argue with yourself about your score. You need to bounce it off someone else.

As shown in Figure 1, I propose that you get a mentor to also fill-in the scorecard. You then would compare and contrast your scoring with the scoring of the mentor. If you have more than one mentor, do the same with each of them. You can also try having others fill-in the scorecard, such as other members of your team. Overall, the idea is that you want to collect feedback, and the scorecard provides a structured way to do so.

For each of the scores on each element, see how close and how far apart you are from those others that also do the scoring. What does the gap tell you? Maybe you are deluding yourself about some elements of the startup. Maybe you have not communicated about some elements and so those around you don't know what you know. Either way, it can be revealing.

I sometimes use a simple radar chart to depict the scorecard scores. Take a look at Figure 2. Here, I show my score as a mentor and the score of a founder that I was helping.

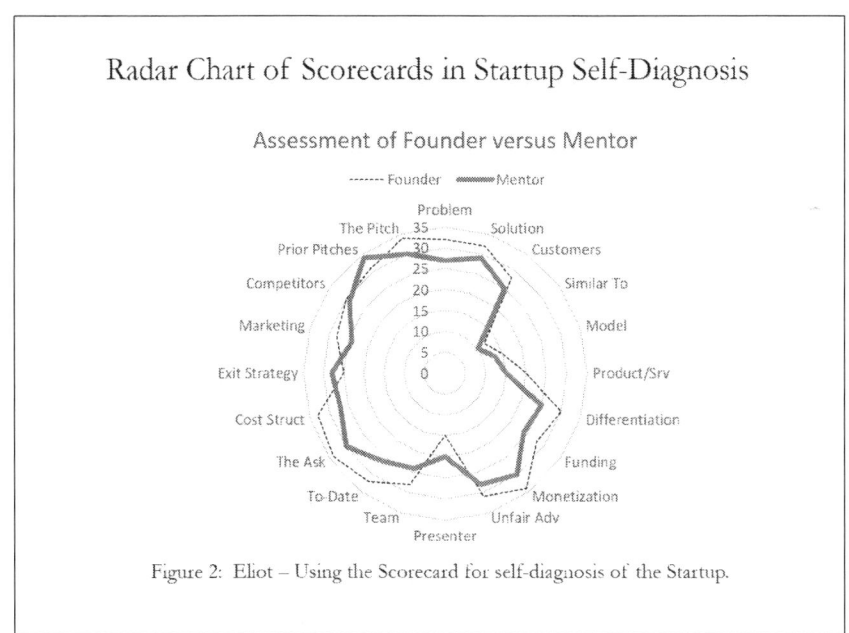

Figure 2: Eliot – Using the Scorecard for self-diagnosis of the Startup.

You can see that we were relatively close on our respective scoring of her startup. On the elements of "The Ask" and the "To-Date" it was my view that she did not have a strong ask in-hand and nor that her to-date was as accomplished as she thought. We discussed this aspect in-depth. As a "Presenter" I gave her better marks than what she gave herself. She was the type of person that felt she was not that good a presenter. I agreed that she wasn't great at presenting, but was better than what she self-scored herself.

It is interesting to notice that we were pretty close on the scores. I say that because often this exercise reveals some dramatic differences. In this case, because I had been working closely with the founder, we were already quite aligned. You should prepare yourself to discover to your surprise, and often times to your dismay, the others that fill-in the scorecard might be very afield of your scores. That's fine, and gives you lots to discuss with them. This will likely lead to adjustments or pivoting.

PREDICTING THE JUDGE SCORES AND SCALING

The other aspect of using the scorecard involves trying to predict the scores that the judges will assign you. After you have prepared the first draft of your pitch, do the pitch for someone that can fill-in the scorecard while pretending to be a judge. This person should preferably be someone that has business startup expertise. If you have your young son or daughter fill-in the scorecard, it probably won't be as impactful on your startup, though they and you might certainly enjoy it and the experience could be a family bonding moment (or, I suppose, cause a family rift!).

One difficulty in filling in the form has to do with the scale. The scale allows for a score of 1 to 5 on each element. The 1 is low, the 5 is high, and a zero is used if you do not say anything at all about an element. I usually suggest giving a 1 on every element that is at least covered in the pitch. Some judges aren't quite so kind, and they like to give a zero if the element is covered but they believe that the coverage was worthless.

There will be hardnosed judges that will give nearly all 1's, no matter what the pitch is about. There are softy judges that will give nearly all 5's, no matter what the pitch is about. It can be like the Olympics, where the Russian judge gives a high score and the American judge a low score, and vice versa on other pitches.

Some judges will instantly score higher if the problem area is something that they know, such as suppose a judge has expertise in mobile app related startups and the participant is showcasing a mobile app. Of course it can go the other way, wherein a mobile app versed judge might be very harsh on any participant that is pitching a mobile app, since the judge knows what is good and what is not, presumably.

It is up to the judges to hopefully try and figure out how each other judge is using the scale. I usually suggest to my fellow judges that we all reserve a score of 5 for only instances wherein the element really was truly outstanding. The score of 3 means that it is average in comparison to other startups and pitches. A score of 1 means that the element was touched upon but appears to have not much backing to it. The score of 4 and 2 are then in-between the middle and the top and the bottom.

Once the judges get into the deliberation, there is often a lot of scoring changes made by the judges, doing so to settle down upon a group kind of consensus on the scoring. The key is that the judges will want to at least support whatever scores they use, and then make sure that there is a level playing field. For a judge that gives every element a 1 no matter what, they aren't going to have much of a total score for the participants. This comes out quickly and then the judges tend to re-calibrate after-the-fact. Some events ask the judges to do this calibration before the event starts.

A difficulty with doing the calibration before the event will be that the judges might be thinking of absolutes. For example, suppose they decide that a 5 can only be earned if the element is "world class" for that startup. As I have mentioned earlier in this book, the pitch competition is really taking place on a *relative basis* to the other participants, and not occurring on an absolute basis. If the judges try to use an absolute scale, it might be problematic.

Allow me to offer an example. I was at a local pitch competition that had startups that were really (politely stated) stitched together. These were founders that were pure newbies to starting a business. A week before, I had been a judge at a pitch competition that consisted of graduates from a recognized university entrepreneurship program. They were all polished and seasoned entrepreneurs. Trying to score based on them would have been problematic for the competition of the newbies. We would have had to score the newbies nearly all 1's, since the other competition was so far above where they were in startup maturity. This would have not been a very useful way to differentiate among the startups at this particular pitch competition.

So, when you try to do a self-diagnosis, and when you have others do the same for you, the odds are that you'll need to do a similar kind of exercise in terms of agreeing to the nature of how to use the scale. Trying to predict what the actual judges will score can be hard without having a sense of your competition that will appear at the startup pitch event, but it is worthwhile anyway as an exercise in preparation.

Finally, you might consider using the scorecard at a competition. While watching the other participants as they give their pitches, score them. This might help you get a relative sense of where they are, and allow you to consider making on-the-fly adjustments to your pitch as befits the relative circumstances.

CHAPTER 6

FALSEHOODS ABOUT YOUR PITCH APPROACH

CHAPTER 6

FALSEHOODS ABOUT YOUR
PITCH APPROACH

PREFACE

I hear things. Don't be worried, there aren't voices in my head. The things I hear at startup pitch competitions often involves "sage advice" being given to startup pitch participants. Someone that claims to have all-knowledge of startup pitches will tell a newbie that they must do certain things and must not do other certain things. When I hear this so-called advice, it sometimes makes me shudder because it is often completely misleading or outright wrong.

The falsehoods told to a startup pitch participant can cause the participant to get even more nervous due to the aspect that they are thinking now about how and whether or not to abide by the advice. Furthermore, if they do abide by the oddball advice, the odds are that it will undermine their startup pitch rather than enhance it. Imagine that you have practiced your pitch over and over, and at the last minute you get advice that seems to be coming from a credible source. You are in a quandary if you have violated that advice, and must decide whether to make last desperate changes to your pitch. I share with you some of the falsehoods to give you a sense of what to watch out for.

———————

CHAPTER 6: FALSEHOODS ABOUT YOUR PITCH APPROACH

You should hop on one leg, wave your right arm, and whistle a tune to make sure your startup pitch at a competition will be the winning pitch. Well, I am just pulling your leg on that. I hear others giving advice to startup founders about how and what they should do in their startup pitches for competitions. Often, the advice is just about as good as the aforementioned hopping, waving, and whistling. In other words, I find much of the so-called sage advice to be misguiding and downright wrong.

Somehow, you need to discern between useful advice and useless advice. It can be hard to discern the differences. If someone that has done pitches offers you advice, you are likely to assume it is worthwhile. If a judge or mentor gives advice, you assume it must be good. There are lots of varying perspectives about how to do a startup pitch. You will hear many suggestions. I'd like to take a moment and point out some blatantly false ones that seem to keep spreading like a virus.

Figure 1 shows the falsehoods that I am going to address. I offer in the chart a quick retort as to why the falsehood is false.

Falsehoods About Your Pitch Approach

	Falsehoods about Pitching	Corrections about Pitching
1	"Never use video in your pitch"	It is OK to use video, wisely
2	"Shortest pitch is the winner"	Right-size your pitch, not shortest
3	"No slickness should be used"	Slick is good if not overplayed
4	"End stronger than you start"	Bookend strong start & strong end
5	"Always keep it simple"	Simple is good, complex at times OK
6	"Never display arrogance"	Arrogance can be used for effect
7	"Don't waste time on your journey"	Journey can be powerful, use well
8	"Aim for a big laugh"	Humor is dicey, be very careful

Figure 1: Eliot – Falsehoods about pitching and corrections.

Incorrect Advice: "Never use video in your pitch"

Correct Advice: It is OK to use video, wisely

This first example of bad advice is one of my all-time favorites as bad advice. It keeps going round and round. The stickiness of it is amazing. Anyway, the advice given is that you should never use video in your pitch. The basis for this advice is that by showing video you are taking away the judges attention from you, and you presumably want them riveted on you. You are the star. You are the person that they are judging. Therefore, if you show a video, it will take away from the time that is already limited for them to see you and judge you.

As an argument for the falsehood, I certainly can see why the rationale is very compelling. But, I think the advice is misleading and tosses the baby out with the bath water. I assert that it can be Okay to use video, but only if it is used wisely. I will explain in much detail what I mean by wisely using video.

First, the impact that a good video can have is tremendous. A picture is worth a thousand words, and video is thousands of such words. In a very brief amount of time, a well-produced video can make apparent what you might be struggling to say. A video can get past the outer hardened shell of the judges and pierce into their soul. It can make quite memorable what your startup is about. It can standout since most rarely use video, partially due to the advice being given to not do so. That makes it an opportunity for you.

That being the case, video is a dual edged sword. If you show a video that is cheap looking and confusing, it will do more damage than help. If the video does not actually explain your startup and its gist, you will be undermining your pitch. The video has to be professionally done, aimed at what you are as a startup, succinct, catching, and be an integrated part of your pitch. You don't want to just suddenly blurt out "let's go to video" and also when the video is done you need to immediately take hold of the pitch once again.

If you cannot do the above, then I say don't do video. I am saying don't do it not because video is inherently bad, but only if the video is badly done. You will need to figure out how much of your pitch time you can devote to the video. It should be only a fraction like say a fourth or less of your time. You also cannot waste time getting the video to start and end, so if you the logistics at the event isn't going to allow the video to be shown well, don't do it.

That's actually the biggest issue usually about video. Not many of the startup pitch competitions are able to accommodate video. They don't have a sizable screen, they don't have the judges and audience in a position to be able to see the screen, the sound systems is lousy, etc. If any of those logistics aspects are in the way of doing video, I say don't do video. Probably not even worth trying to do it.

The only times to do the video are either when you know that you have good video and that it logistically can be shown properly, or when an event states that they want to have video. If the event itself is telling you to show video, and you don't show video, the odds are that not complying will make you look worse.

Incorrect Advice: "Shortest pitch is the winner"

Correct Advice: Right-size your pitch, not shortest

My next most favorite piece of bad advice that I hear is the notion that the shortest pitch will be the winner of a startup pitch competition. Sounds compelling as advice. Short and sweet, as they say. I would like to debunk this one.

Most pitches will use the same amount of time, which is whatever amount of time was allotted by the event. Suppose that the pitch is allowed to be 3 minutes in length. The judges are expecting to see 3 good minutes. They know that you cannot possibly cover everything in just 3 minutes, and so they expect it to be reasonably jam packed and that you will likely go right up to the 3 minute timer.

There is often a moderator that will cut you off at the stated time limit. Try not to be in the middle of saying something really important, since it looks bad that you did not use your time well. You should be winding down your pitch as you get to the end of the stated time limit, rather than winding up or trying to cram in more stuff. Remember too that usually there is a Q&A after your canned pitch, and so you can use the Q&A portion to cover other aspects that you wanted to include in the canned part.

Let's now consider the advice about being the shortest pitch in order to win. If you went for say one minute in a pitch that could go three minutes, the judges would be taken aback. You had two additional minutes and did not use them. It is hard to imagine that in the one minute that you covered all key factors about the startup. It will seem that you either are ill-prepared or misunderstand how you should use the time involved in the pitch.

You should right-size your pitch. It should use all of the available pitch time for the canned portion, but not with any fluff. If you genuinely cannot think of anything important to say and want to end a little bit early that's certainly fine. But the shortest pitch says nothing about the chances of winning and usually an aberrantly short pitch is a bad sign.

Incorrect Advice: "No slickness should be used"

Correct Advice: Slick is good if not overplayed

The next bad advice to debunk involves the claim that you should not be slick in your pitch. Let's unpack that notion. Slick means different things to different people. If by being slick it is meant that you are a sleazy sales person that oozes insincerity and treats your audience and the judges like dolts, I agree that you should not be "slick" in that sense of the word.

I think that most people giving this advice are doing so to emphasize that today's proper sense of pitches is that you are to give a pitch from the heart. You are to be an authentic founder and leader. We eschew the crassness of the old ways in which a sales type pitch would be given. No more selling of swamp land in Florida by brow beating others.

By the way, make no bones about it, your startup pitch is a sales pitch. You need to have a polished pitch that does not smell or appear to be a slickly done sales pitch. Without some amount of slickness, though, the odds are that it implies your pitch will be poorly prepared. If you look overly practiced and act like a robot, it will lessen the sense that this is your business and that you care about the business. If you look entirely stilted and cannot communicate about the startup, even if it is a great business, we might not know that it is. Find the right balance.

Incorrect Advice: "End stronger than you start"

Correct Advice: Bookend strong start & strong end

This bad advice certainly sounds sensible. It says that you should end more strongly than you start. I suppose there is some truth to this in that if you cannot start strongly then you had better make sure to have a strong end.

Why can't you have a very strong start and a very strong end? I say you can. I say you should strive for it. There is nothing mutually exclusive about starting strong and then also ending strong. They are like two bookends, both can be equally strong.

Some founders think that if they start less strongly, it will lessen expectations and allow them to really shine with a strong end. The counter argument is that if the start is weak, you can lose the judges right away, and no matter what you do at the end won't be of consequence because your audience has already marked you as DOA and mentally gone elsewhere.

Incorrect Advice: "Always keep it simple"

Correct Advice: Simple is good, complex at times OK

This next piece of bad advice is one that has real legs to it. The adage is that you should always keep thing simple in your pitch. I am certainly in favor of simplifying things. Sometimes, a founder is so steeped in their area of expertise, let's say they are pitching a biomedical device and are a medical physician by training and experience, they will tend to provide a very complex explanation about the product.

A complex explanation can lose some judges. Suppose that you have a judging panel of five judges, of which there are three that are business types that know about startups and financing, while the other two are medical specialists and one has a PhD in biomedicine. In the case of the biomedical device pitch, there are two judges that want the complex stuff. They expect it. Without the complex stuff, they are likely to doubt the veracity of your claims. During the judges deliberations, they will likely be looked to by the other judges and asked whether the product and you are credible. If you have dumb downed things so much that it does not seem credible, you will lose.

Given that the founder in that case was presumably not a business person, the other three judges are willing to give a lot of latitude on the business aspects of the startup. They figure that if the product is good, they can help step in or someone with business savvy can step in and make the business into something. Meanwhile, if the product is not credible, no amount of business savvy is going to get that to bring the startup to life.

I would assert that you should purposely seed into your pitch some amount of complexity as merits the product or service, but only enough to show that you know your stuff. Pitches that use all of their time on being overly complex will probably not go well.

Incorrect Advice: "Never display arrogance"

Correct Advice: Arrogance can be used for effect

We have all seen characters in television and movies that are nerds that act like they are a know-it-all. We have come to expect it. I say this because the next piece of bad advice is to never display arrogance during your pitch.

Believe it or not, if you don't display some arrogance in certain circumstances, the judges will think you aren't as good as you claim. A humble person is not what we have become programmed to look for. We expect that someone of grand expertise will probably be a bit of an annoying person. You can leverage that stereotype to your advantage. Furthermore, don't let that stereotype undermine you by playing against it and being only humble.

There are levels of arrogance to be considered. I doubt that if you walk up to do the pitch and tell the judges that you are the walking messiah on earth, it will help you. This extreme level of arrogance is going to bite you, unless you somehow are there to pitch your startup that cures cancer and solves world hunger.

Incorrect Advice: "Don't waste time on your journey"

Correct Advice: Journey can be powerful, use well

I hear others that tell a founder to not waste their limited pitch time by talking about their journey to getting the startup underway. The viewpoint of these advice giving people is that it is perhaps interesting and important to you, but that the judges want to know what the problem is, what the solution is, and what your startup is going to accomplish. Just the facts, and nothing but the facts.

The judges and nearly everyone else in the pitch competition has likely had a tough journey getting to a startup. It is the nature of the beast. Your bringing up your journey will likely be interesting and catch the attention and the hearts of the judges. I believe that telling about your journey can be very powerful. It explains why you are doing this startup. Also, when the startup gets bogged down, we want to know what will keep you going, and so the journey you have taken already might explain that inner motivation.

I can just see someone thinking that they will then spend their entire three minutes or whatever the pitch time is, covering their journey. If you do that, you will likely not win. It will hurt you if you take us through when you were born, the hospital birthing process, the first cutting of your teeth, your kindergarten grades, and so on. The amount of the journey told should be relevant and proportional to the telling about the startup.

Incorrect Advice: "Aim for a big laugh"

Correct Advice: Humor is dicey, be very careful

This last falsehood is an easy one to debunk. The advice given is that you should aim for a big laugh during your pitch. If you are a natural comedian and if your startup is the next best comedy club, I suppose you do need to show us that you can make us laugh. Otherwise, trying to use humor in a pitch is very hard to pull off. Have you seen people that try to make a joke and it goes flat? The audience becomes hushed. It can kill whatever buzz you might have had going.

Furthermore, much of the humor that we find funny relies upon using some kind of politically incorrect aspect. Do you want to tell a joke about people's beliefs, and in so doing alienate those that perhaps harbor the beliefs you are ridiculing? Not a good idea. There is not much humor that you can use that won't offend someone. Why needlessly offend someone if it won't really add much anyway?

I know that one "safer" realm of humor in this context is to refer to pitches and competitions. You can maybe try that, but even it could go awry. Suppose your joke insults the organizers of the event? That's not a good idea. Showing that you have a sense of humor can be handy, but trying to be a comedian is not what most judges care about.

FINAL COMMENTS ABOUT FALSEHOODS

There are new falsehoods being minted every day. Be on the watch. Generally, these falsehoods do not need to be adhered to. The exception might that if you participate in a particular pitch competition and they tell you outright one of my above listed falsehoods and indicate you must adhere to it, then I'd say don't try to buck the system and just go along with whatever they say. If they want you to wear party hats and hop on one leg, go for it. More seriously, for example, an event might say "no video allowed" in which case, even if you have a million hits on your YouTube video about your startup, you might want to think twice about using it.

Good luck and make your pitch count!

CHAPTER L1
THE SOLVABLE PROBLEM

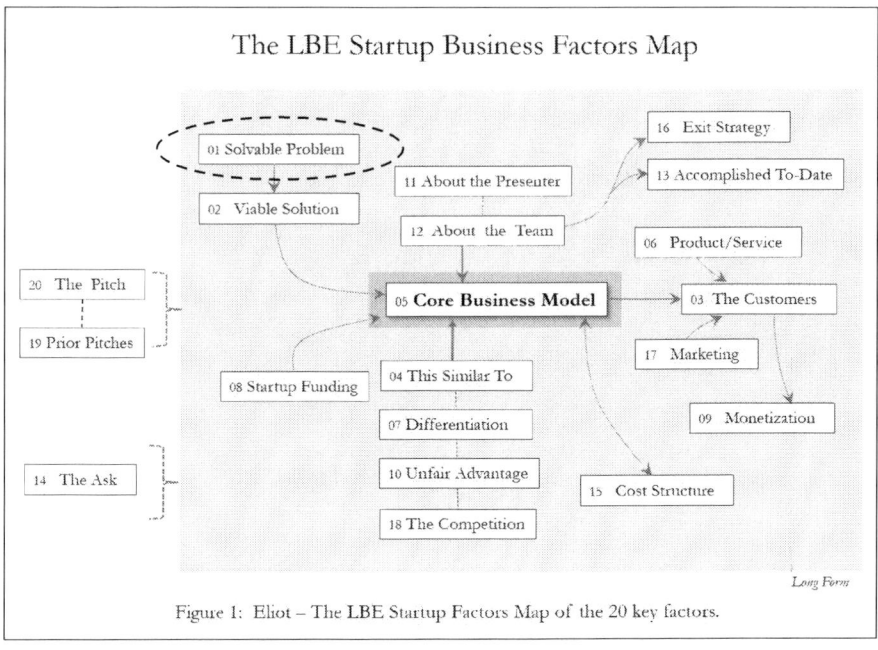

Figure 1: Eliot – The LBE Startup Factors Map of the 20 key factors.

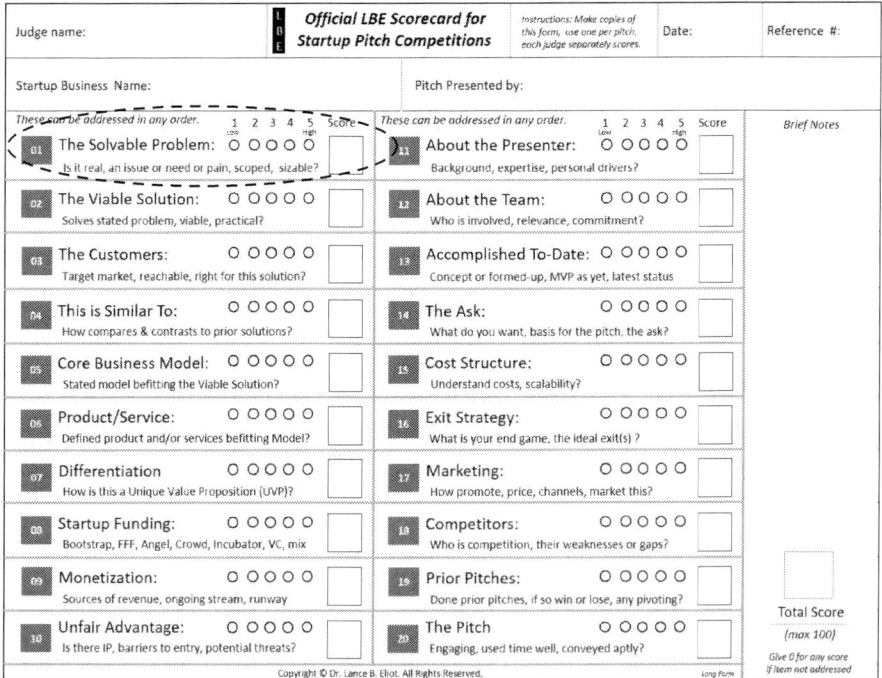

CHAPTER L1
THE SOLVABLE PROBLEM

What This Is:

Your startup needs to be shaped around some kind of business solvable problem. Maybe the problem is that Americans are getting obese and this is leading to higher healthcare costs, illnesses, and even early death. That is a problem that judges can instantly understand. Whatever problem you identify, it should be real, it should be clearly comprehensible as a true issue or need or pain. And, you will also need to be able to offer a viable solution (in element L2). It should be sizable if you want to attract earnest investors.

Why Is It Important:

Nothing else about your startup will make much sense without having identified a solvable problem. The startup exists in order to solve the stated problem. If you don't have a stated problem then there is no meaningful purpose presumably for your business.

Questions You Will be Asked:

o   What is the problem you are trying to solve?
o   Can you succinctly state the actual issue, need, or pain?
o   Why did you pick that particular problem?
o   How big is the problem in terms of being widespread?
o   What makes you believe that this problem exists?
o   Has anyone else also identified this problem?
o   Have you personally experienced the problem?

Typical Scoring Scale:

0 = Did not address the problem
1 = Mentioned the problem vaguely
2 = Described the problem but it seems insignificant
3 = Problem was described and it seems valid
4 = Really well understands the problem and it is bona fide
5 = Great problem that has strong potential for a startup

CHAPTER L2

THE VIABLE SOLUTION

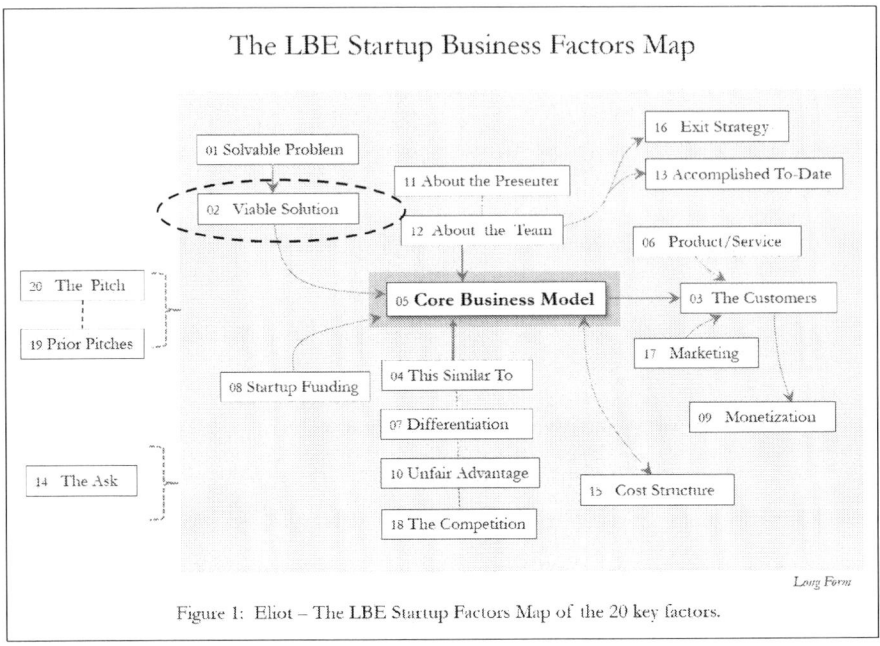

Figure 1: Eliot – The LBE Startup Factors Map of the 20 key factors.

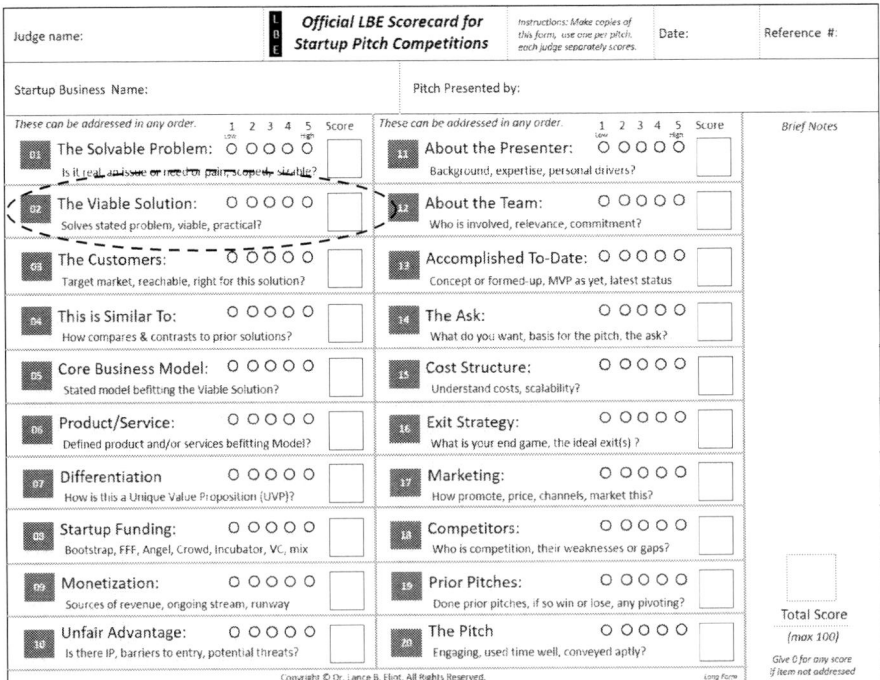

CHAPTER L2
THE VIABLE SOLUTION

What This Is:

> Your startup needs to offer a viable solution to whatever solvable business problem you indicated in L1. If the solvable problem was the advent of obesity in America, your solution should then correspondingly solve that problem. Your solution needs to be viable. For example, it would *not* be viable to say that obesity would be solved by clamping shut the mouths of all Americans. Whatever solution you propose, it should be real, it should be clearly comprehensible as a means to reduce, alleviate, or eliminate the issue or need or pain. It should be a solution that is desired by a sizable part of your market.

Why Is It Important:

> Nothing else about your startup will make much sense without having identified a viable solution. The startup exists in order to enact the stated solution. If you don't have a stated solution then there is no meaningful purpose presumably for your business.

Questions You Will be Asked:

- o   What is the solution you are proposing?
- o   In what way is the solution viable?
- o   Have others tried to use that same solution?
- o   What has prevented this solution from already being used?
- o   Can you succinctly state the solution?
- o   What will make your solution successful?

Typical Scoring Scale:

- 0 = Did not identify the solution
- 1 = Mentioned the solution vaguely
- 2 = Described the solution but it seems not viable
- 3 = Solution was described and it seems viable
- 4 = Really well understands the solution and it is bona fide
- 5 = Great solution that has strong potential for a startup

CHAPTER L3

THE CUSTOMERS

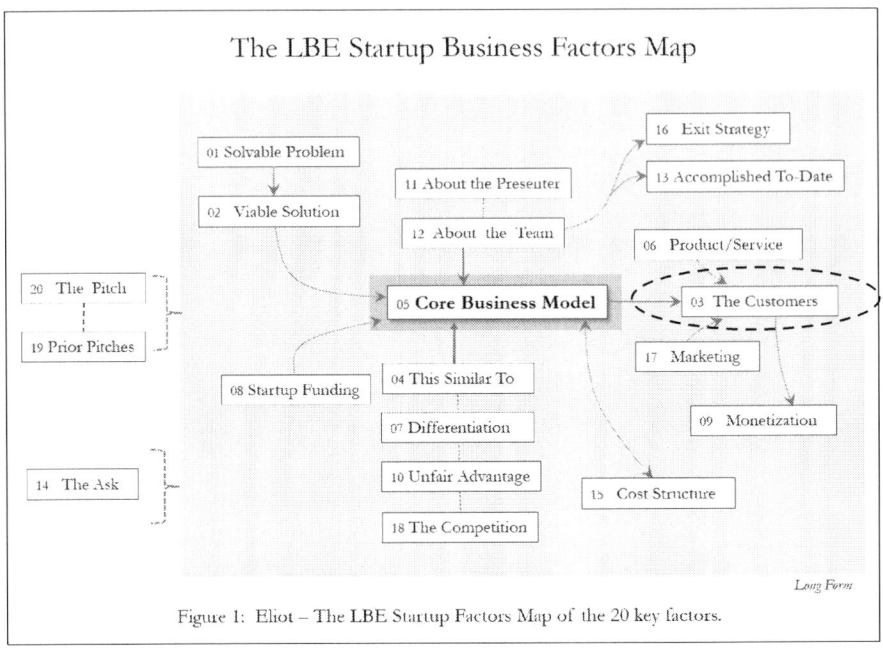

Figure 1: Eliot – The LBE Startup Factors Map of the 20 key factors.

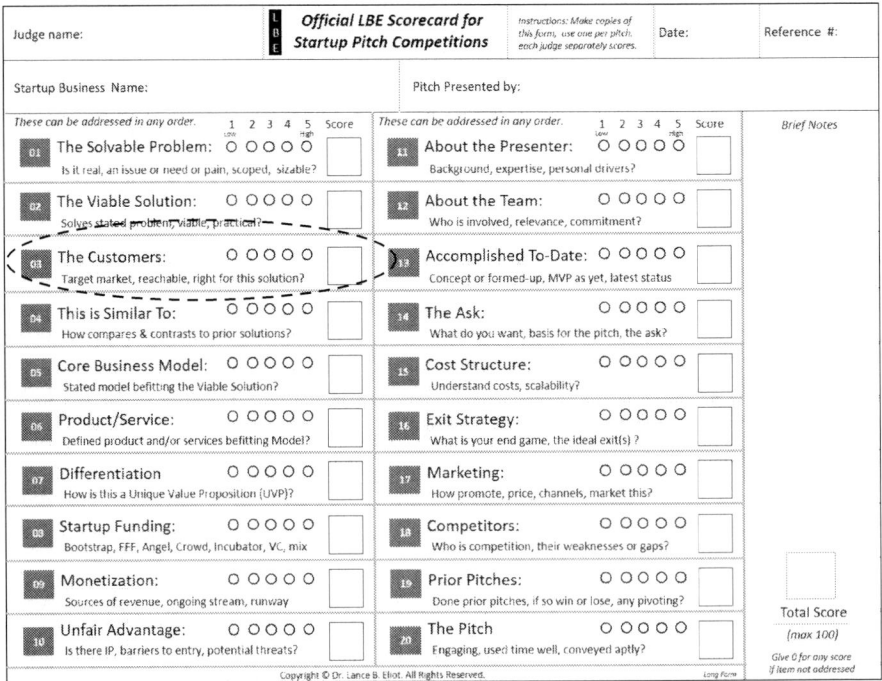

CHAPTER L3
THE CUSTOMERS

What This Is:

> Your startup needs to be able to identify the customers of your viable solution and that presumably are encompassed by the solvable problem. If your solution is about overcoming obesity in America, you would not want to focus on say underweight Russians or Italians. Explain your target market, including how it can be reached and the size and scope of that market.

Why Is It Important:

> You need to have a profile of your customers and be able to show that they have the problem stated in L1. Without focusing on your customers, whatever product or service that you provide as a viable solution will flounder since you don't know what customers will want to use it or buy it, if any.

Questions You Will be Asked:

- o   Who is the customer you are aiming at?
- o   How many are there of these (size of market)?
- o   What is the typical profile of these customer(s)?
- o   In what manner do they have the solvable problem?
- o   In what manner does your viable solution fit to them?
- o   How will you be able to reach these customer(s)?
- o   Are there other solutions already targeting these customer(s)?

Typical Scoring Scale:

0 = Did not address the customer at all
1 = Mentioned the customer vaguely
2 = Described the customer but was ill-defined
3 = Customer was described and a good grasp exists
4 = Really well understands the customer and market
5 = Great customer target with strong potential for a startup

CHAPTER L4

THIS IS SIMILAR TO

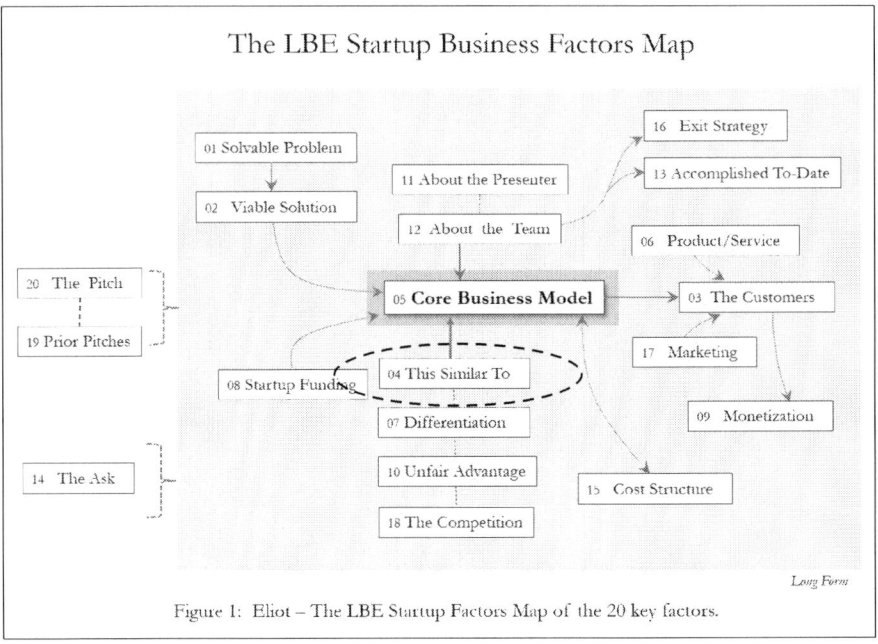

Figure 1: Eliot – The LBE Startup Factors Map of the 20 key factors.

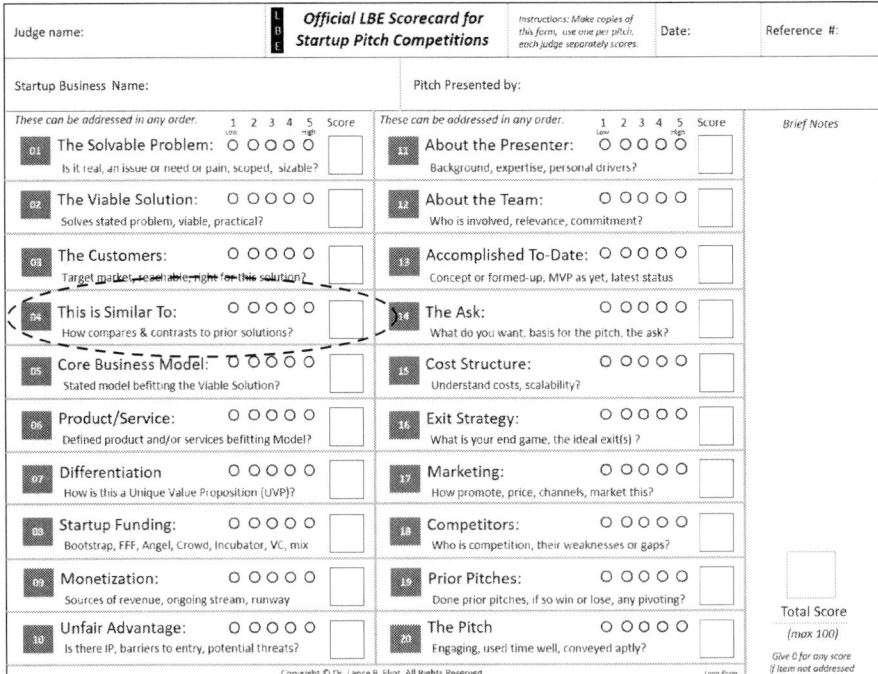

CHAPTER L4
THIS IS SIMILAR TO

What This Is:

> Judges are able to quickly grasp your startup by knowing how it is similar to other business that they might know of. If your solution for obesity in America is to provide a mobile app for weight watching, you could say that your startup is a mash-up of Fitbit and Snapchat. This allows others to immediately comprehend what you are trying to be.

Why Is It Important:

> Just like wanting to know about a new movie that is coming out, we usually want to know what other movie the new one is similar to. By making such a comparison, it reveals quickly whether the movie is a drama, action, kid's film, etc. A startup is the same way. The fastest way to succinctly describe your startup is by providing a similar to.

Questions You Will be Asked:

- o   What is the your startup most like?
- o   How does your startup differ from those other ones?
- o   Have you studied closely those others?
- o   Why wouldn't one of those others squash you?
- o   Are you hoping that one of those others might buy you?
- o   Why do you suppose those others aren't trying to do the same?
- o   Have you considered any other firms that you are similar to?

Typical Scoring Scale:

0 = Did not address the "similar to" aspects
1 = Mentioned the "similar to" vaguely
2 = Described the "similar to" but the others aren't like your startup
3 = The "similar to" was described and it seems valid
4 = Knows well the other similar firms and it is bona fide
5 = Great "similar to's" that has strong potential for a startup

.

CHAPTER L5

CORE BUSINESS MODEL

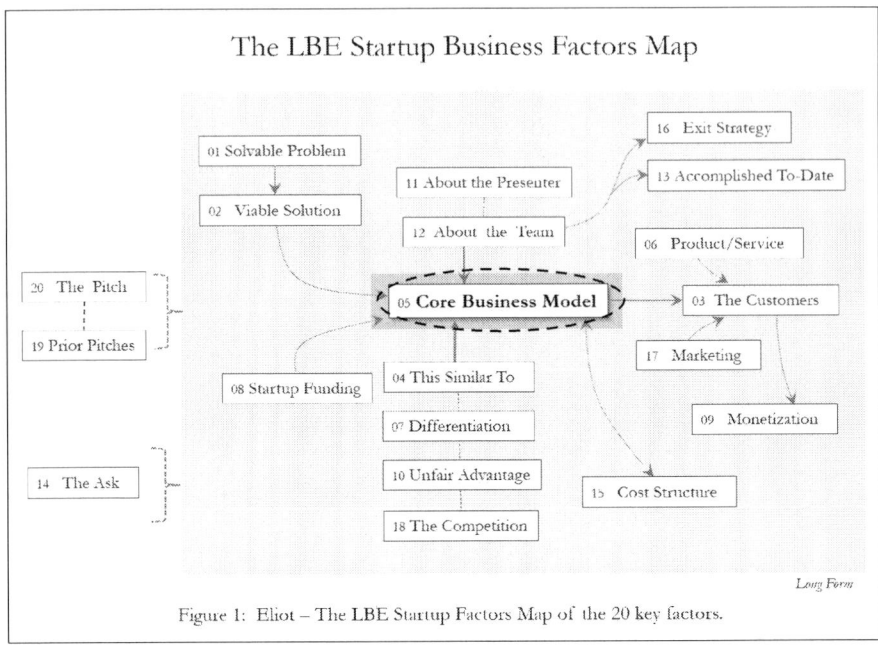

Figure 1: Eliot – The LBE Startup Factors Map of the 20 key factors.

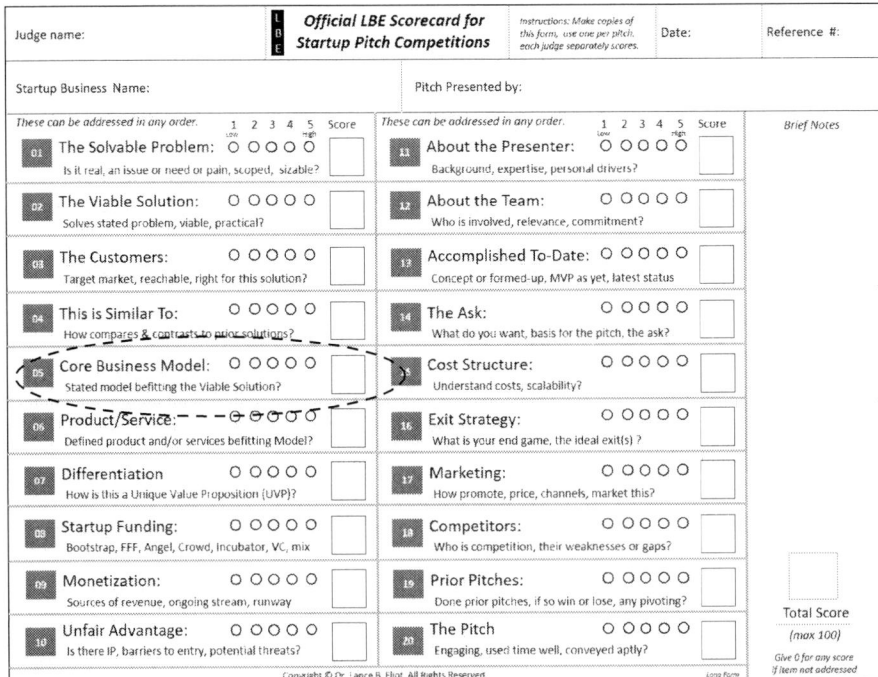

CHAPTER L5
CORE BUSINESS MODEL

What This Is:

Your startup needs a core business model. The core business model identifies how you see the business being shaped to solve the solvable problem and provide the viable solution. For example, you might use an advertising business model, or an auction business model, or a freemium business model, or subscription business model, or a razor and blades business model, etc. If you are providing a mobile app to reduce obesity in the United States, perhaps your core business model involves a combination of the advertising and freemium models.

Why Is It Important:

The core business model indicates what the business consists of, and will dictate the other elements such as your cost structure, your monetization, and so on. It is the backbone of your startup.

Questions You Will be Asked:

- o   What is your core business model?
- o   How did you select that business model?
- o   Has this business model worked in similar firms?
- o   Have you ever been in a firm with this business model?
- o   Do you have advisers or mentors that know this model?
- o   What risks do you see with this business model?

Typical Scoring Scale:

0 = Did not address the core business model at all
1 = Mentioned the core business model vaguely
2 = Described the model but it seems misaligned with this firm
3 = Business model was described and it seems appropriate
4 = Really well understands the model and how to enact it
5 = Great model choice that has strong potential for this startup

CHAPTER L6
PRODUCT/SERVICE

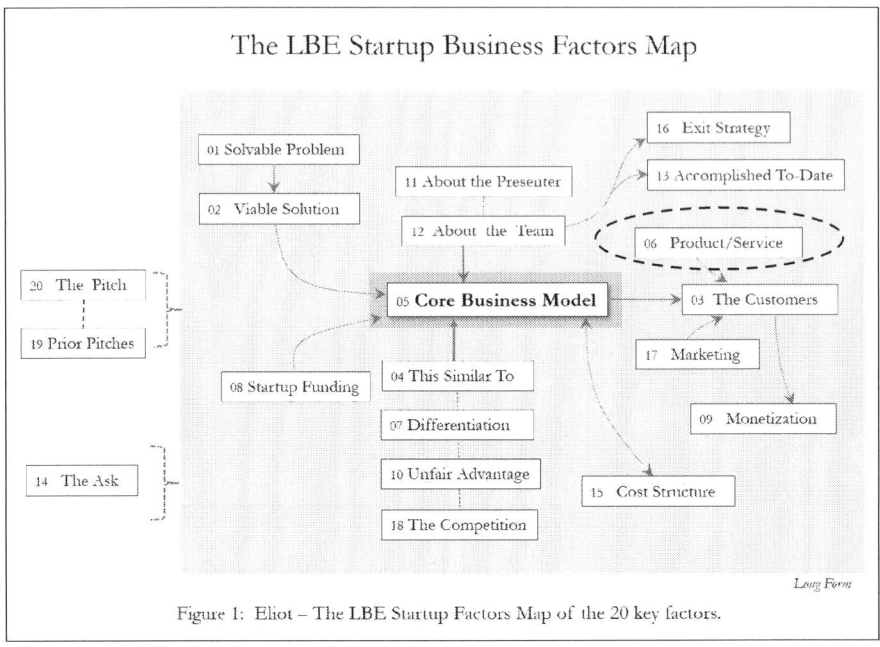

Figure 1: Eliot – The LBE Startup Factors Map of the 20 key factors.

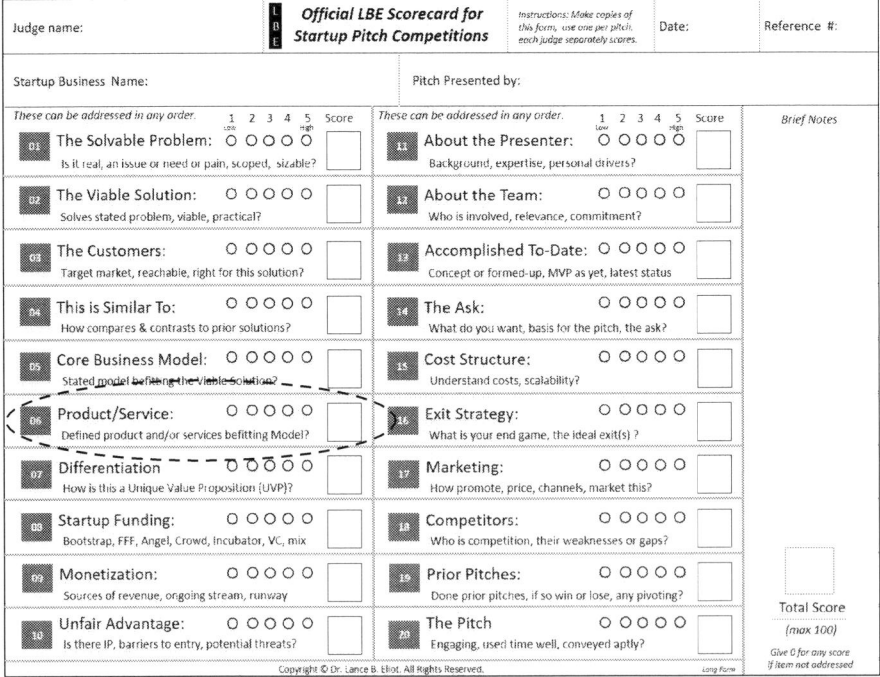

CHAPTER L6
PRODUCT/SERVICE

What This Is:

> Your startup needs to have some kind of products or services that it provides, since how else will your customers obtain the provided viable solution to the solvable problem? You can be product-only focused, you can be service-only focused, or you can have a mixture of both product and service. If you are providing a mobile app to beat obesity, it would seem to be a product. If you also offered a subscription and dietitians for advising, it would also be a service.

Why Is It Important:

> The judges need to know what your intended product is, or what your intended service is. For products, if you can provide a sketch or a prototype it will help quite a bit in showing what it is, and also that it is feasible to produce. For services, you need to be able to articulate what the service is, how it is consumed, and how it will be provided.

Questions You Will be Asked:

- o What is the product that you are going to provide?
- o What is the service that you are going to provide?
- o How feasible is it to provide either the product or service?
- o In what manner does the product or service solve the problem?
- o Who else provides the same or similar product/service?
- o Why isn't there already this product/service in the market?
- o What risks do you see with this product/service?

Typical Scoring Scale:

0 = Did not address the product/service at all
1 = Mentioned the product/service vaguely
2 = Described the product/service but it does not fit the problem
3 = Product/service was described and it seems bona fide
4 = The product/service is above par and viable
5 = Very innovative and has strong potential for a startup

CHAPTER L7

DIFFERENTIATION

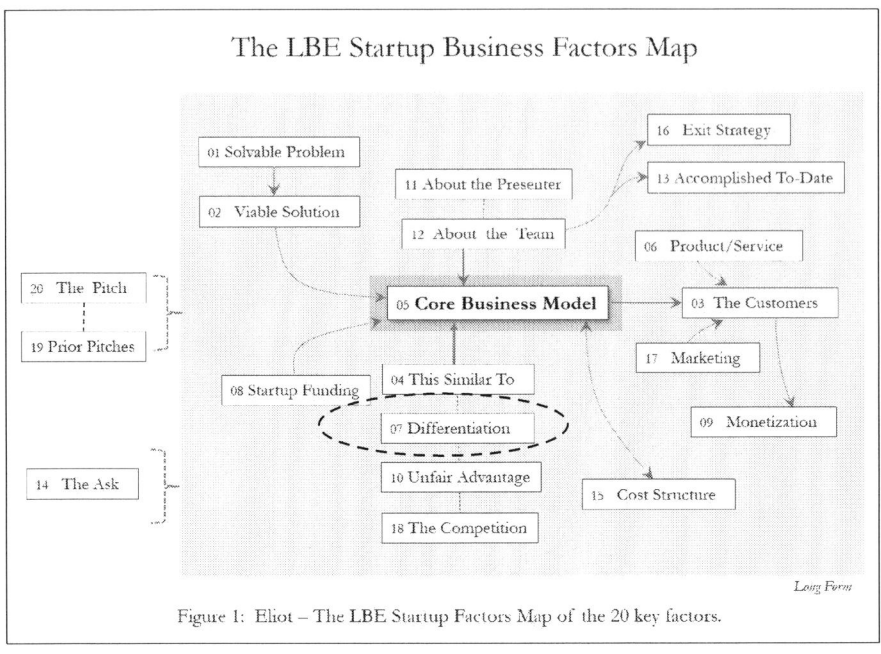

Figure 1: Eliot – The LBE Startup Factors Map of the 20 key factors.

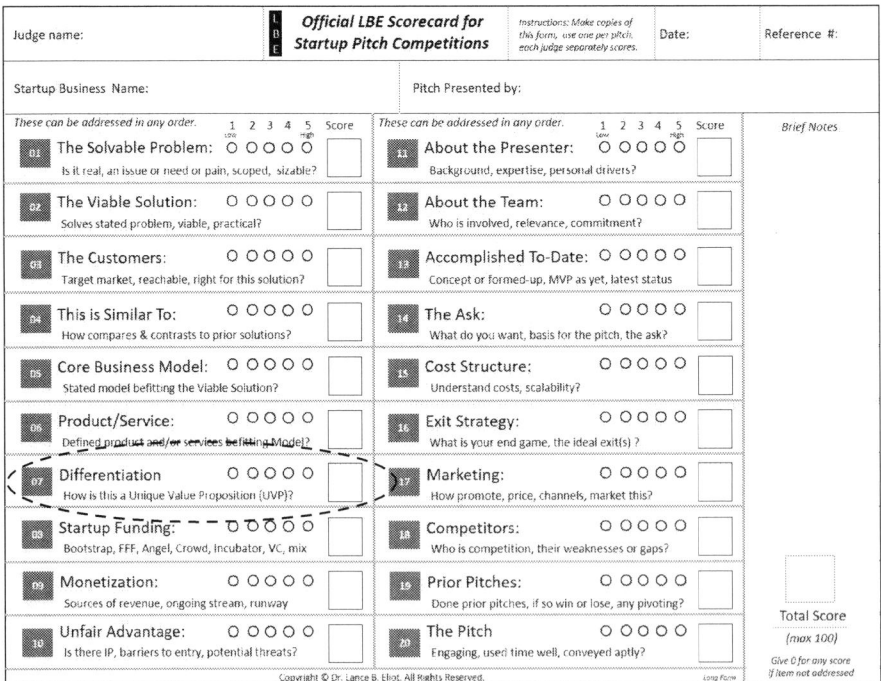

CHAPTER L7
DIFFERENTIATION

What This Is:

Your startup might be just like many others. What is your differentiation? In today's parlance, we ask what is your Unique Value Proposition (UVP)? Somehow, your firm should have a solution composed of your products and services that provides a unique value to your targeted customers.

Why Is It Important:

If your startup is providing a "me too" product or service, it will be hard to get customers to come over to you. They won't perceive any unique value that speaks to them. Your customers will keep doing whatever they are doing now, or doing nothing. Your value proposition is at the heart of the viable solution and core business model.

Questions You Will be Asked:

- o   What is your Unique Value Proposition (UVP)?
- o   How does this UVP compare to other like firms?
- o   In what way does your solution embody the UVP?
- o   In what way do your products/services imbue the UVP?
- o   How does the core business model leverage the UVP?
- o   Have you adjusted the UVP during your startup to-date?
- o   What risks are there associated with having this UVP?

Typical Scoring Scale:

0 = Did not address the UVP
1 = Mentioned the UVP vaguely
2 = Described the UVP but it seems insignificant
3 = UVP was described and it seems valid
4 = Really well understands the UVP and it is bona fide
5 = Great UVP that has strong potential for a startup

CHAPTER L8
STARTUP FUNDING

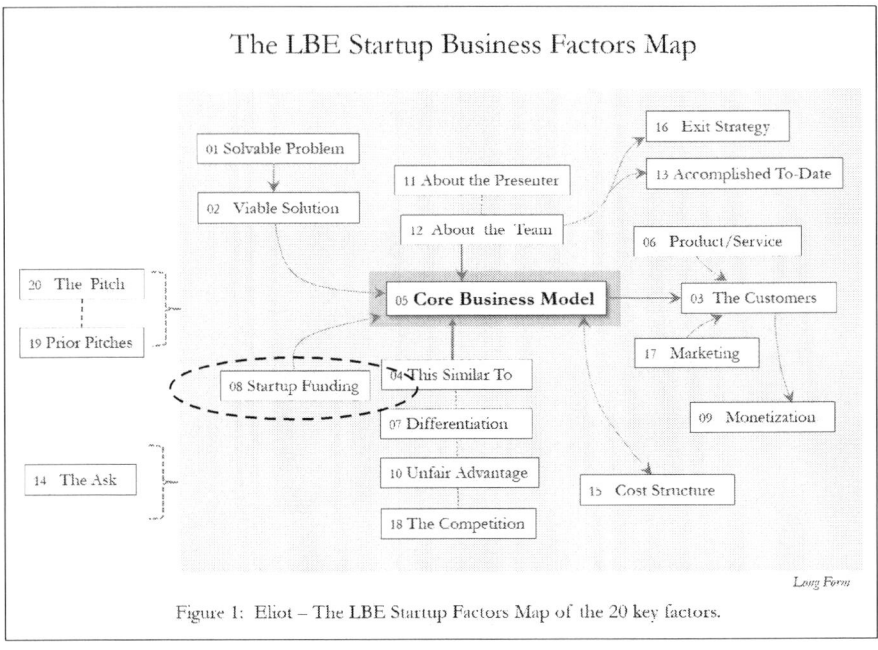

Figure 1: Eliot – The LBE Startup Factors Map of the 20 key factors.

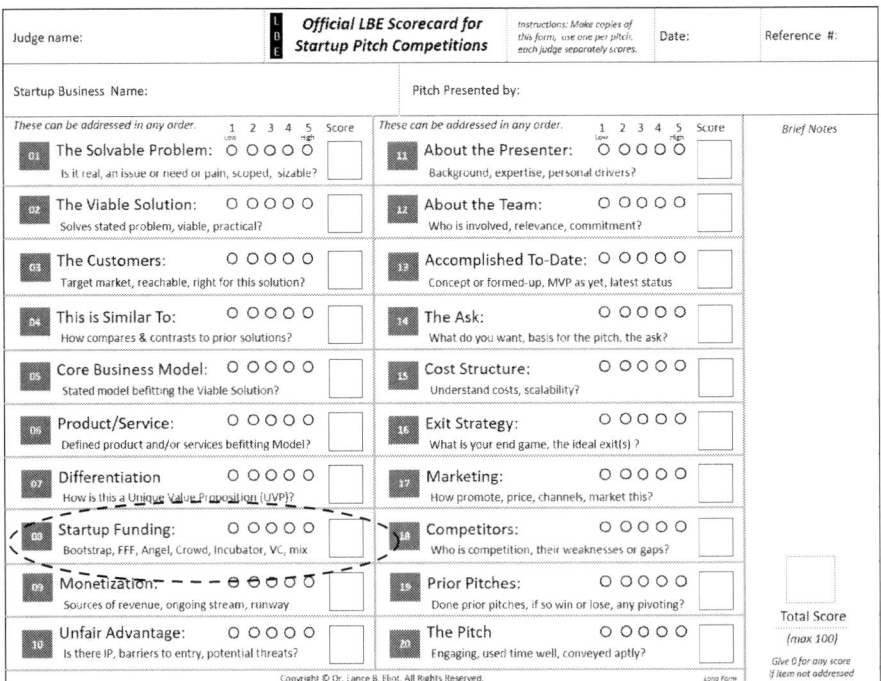

CHAPTER L8
STARTUP FUNDING

What This Is:

Money makes the world go around. Generally, a startup is nothing more than a concept without funding to get it underway. The judges want to know what kind of funding you have already obtained. What sources did you use? And, how have you used the funding and whether you are spending the precious funding properly and wisely.

Why Is It Important:

Funding is the fuel that drives your startup. Most startups collapse because they did not have sufficient funding. The "burn rate" of the startup needs to be understood and a sufficient "runway" of funds needs to be available to get the startup off the ground.

Questions You Will be Asked:

- o   What funding have you obtained for the startup?
- o   Did you "bootstrap" with your own funds (if so, how much)?
- o   Have you used the infamous FFF (family, friends, fools) for funds?
- o   Have you tapped into any angel investors?
- o   Have you considered crowdfunding?
- o   Have you used any incubators, accelerators, or Venture Capital (VC's) for your funding?
- o   How have you been using the funds and how much is left?

Typical Scoring Scale:

0 = Did not address the funding topic
1 = Mentioned the funding vaguely
2 = Described the funding but it seems woefully deficient
3 = Funding was described and it seems suitable for now
4 = Has the needed capital and able to tap into more
5 = Strongly funded and has an excellent runway for a startup

CHAPTER L9

MONETIZATION

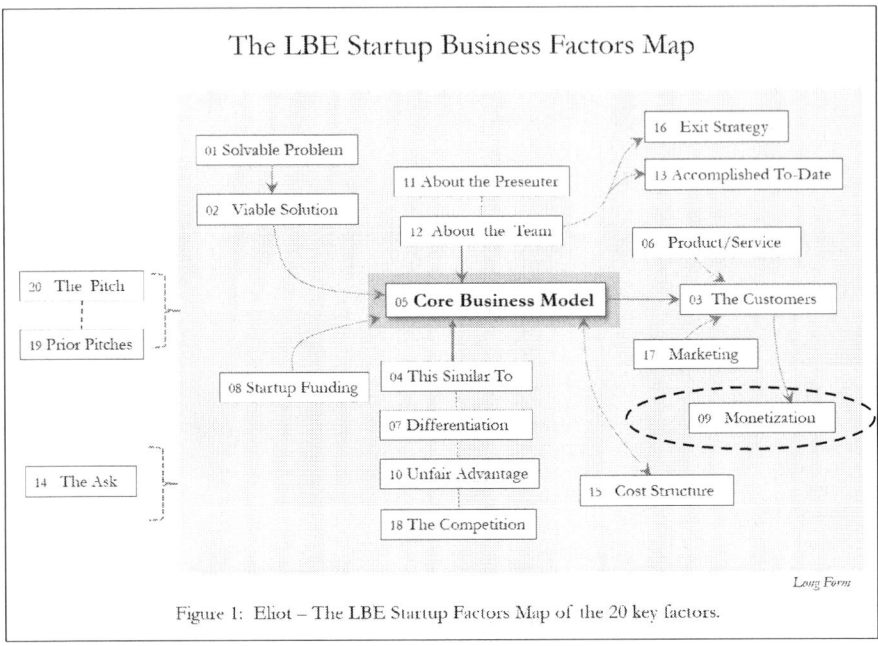

Figure 1: Eliot – The LBE Startup Factors Map of the 20 key factors.

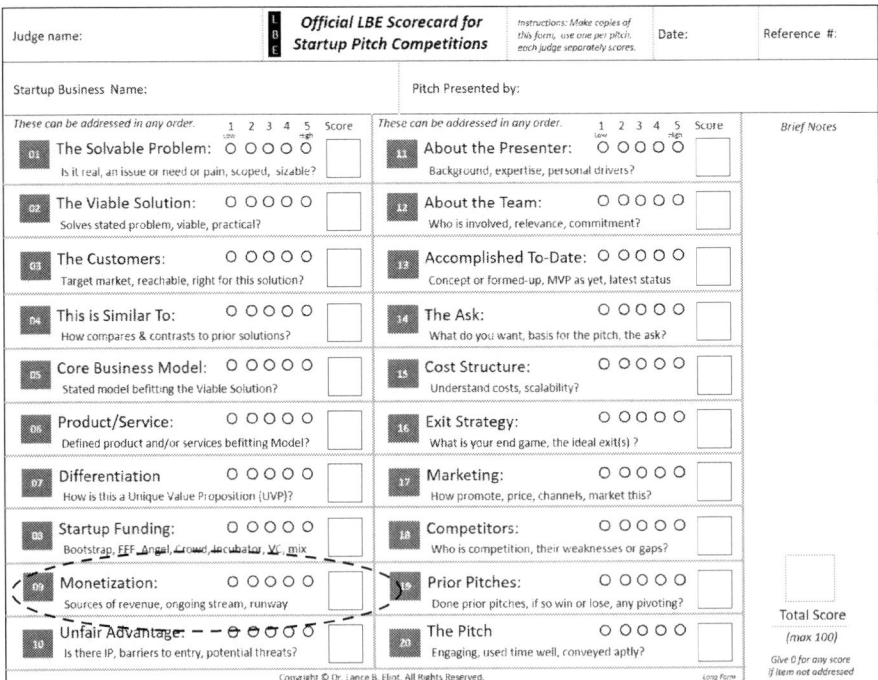

CHAPTER L9

MONETIZATION

What This Is:

> Your startup will ultimately need to make money. Admittedly, there are a lot of tech startups that seem to be able to get away for a long time without actually making money or turning a profit. Anyway, somehow you need to be able to show that eventually and ultimately the startup will make money and be profitable.

Why Is It Important:

> Generally, the sooner your firm makes money then the less reliant it will be on other sources of funding. The firm will be able to shape its own future more readily. Your products or services need to have some path toward bringing in revenue, or in today's parlance we say that you need to be able to "monetize" your products or services.

Questions You Will be Asked:

- o What is your approach to monetizing your products/services?
- o How did you arrive at the numbers you came up with?
- o Are your monetization ideas viable and reasonable?
- o What have you done to test this with your target market?
- o Can you produce the products/services at a cost below the revenue and turn a profit?
- o What risks do you see about your monetization approach?

Typical Scoring Scale:

- 0 = Did not address the monetization
- 1 = Mentioned the monetization vaguely
- 2 = Described the monetization but it seems muddled and unlikely
- 3 = Monetization was described and it seems valid
- 4 = Sound monetization with tangible support as evidence
- 5 = Tested monetization that has strong potential for the startup

CHAPTER L10
UNFAIR ADVANTAGE

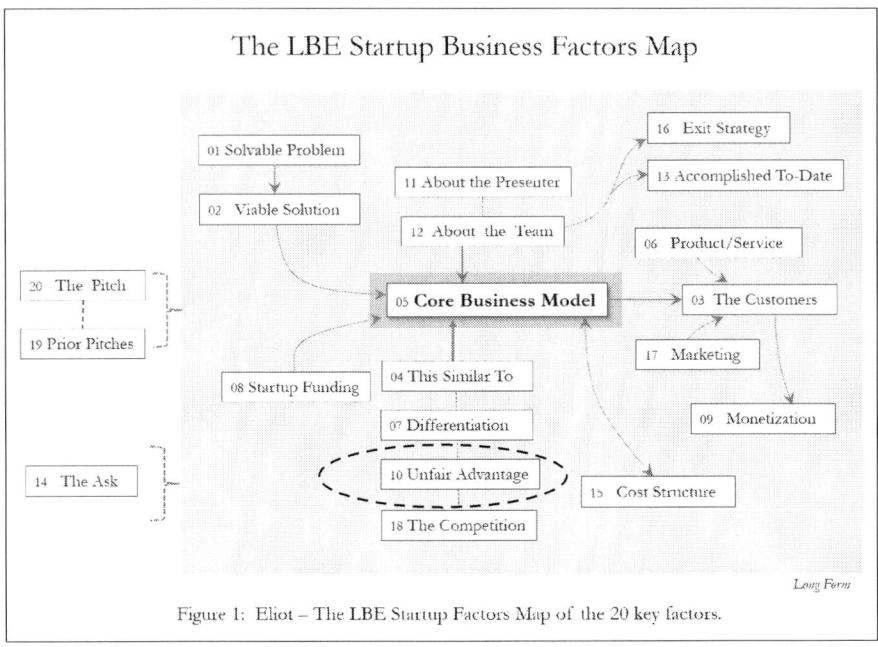

Figure 1: Eliot – The LBE Startup Factors Map of the 20 key factors.

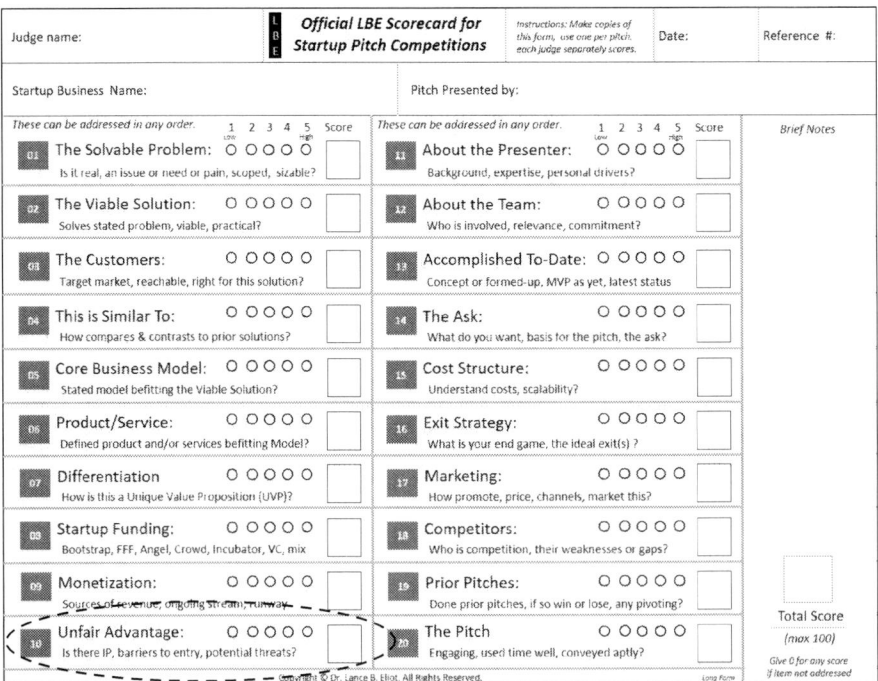

CHAPTER L10
UNFAIR ADVANTAGE

What This Is:

Your startup should strive toward having something that no one else has <u>and</u> equally importantly that you can somehow prevent others from readily duplicating. In today's parlance, this is called an "unfair advantage" over your competition. It is considered "unfair" in that the playing field won't be level and you will have a distinct advantage over them. It is fair to have an unfair advantage, if you can find one.

Why Is It Important:

Without having an unfair advantage, the odds are that the moment you find success there will be ten other firms that jump into your market. You can sometimes have "barriers to entry" that make it hard or costly for competitors to do what you do. For example, you might get a patent on your Intellectual Property (IP) associated with say a mobile app that you are using to reduce obesity.

Questions You Will be Asked:

- o   What is your unfair advantage?
- o   How sustainable is your unfair advantage?
- o   What is the cost to secure your unfair advantage?
- o   How come no one else already has it?
- o   Can your competitors get around your unfair advantage?
- o   Will customers perceive that you do have an unfair advantage?

Typical Scoring Scale:

0 = Did not address the unfair advantage at all
1 = Mentioned the unfair advantage vaguely
2 = Described the unfair advantage but it seems not a true advantage
3 = Unfair advantage was described and it seems viable
4 = Has a clear path to gaining the stated unfair advantage
5 = The unfair advantage is already secured for the startup

CHAPTER L11

ABOUT THE PRESENTER

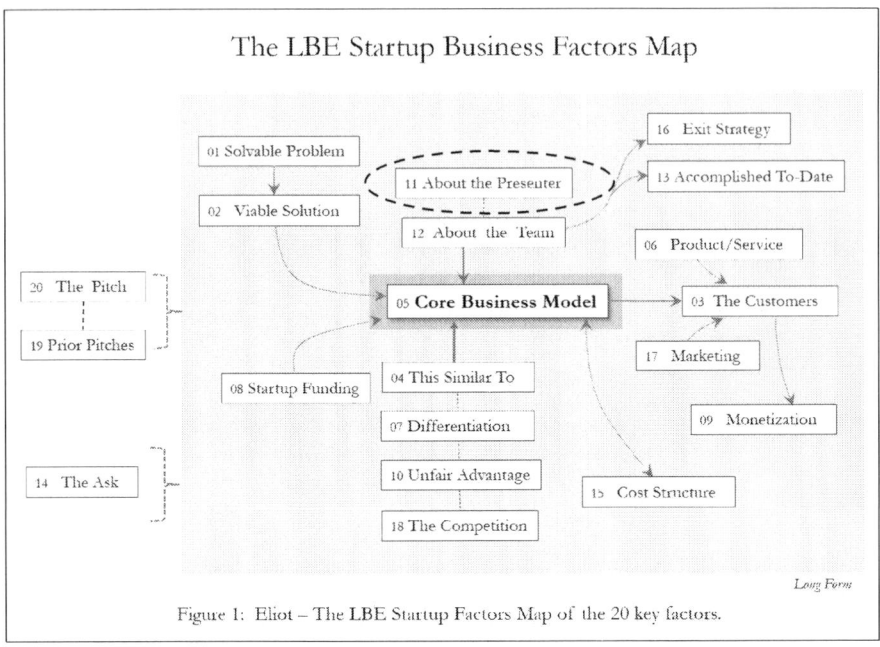

Figure 1: Eliot – The LBE Startup Factors Map of the 20 key factors.

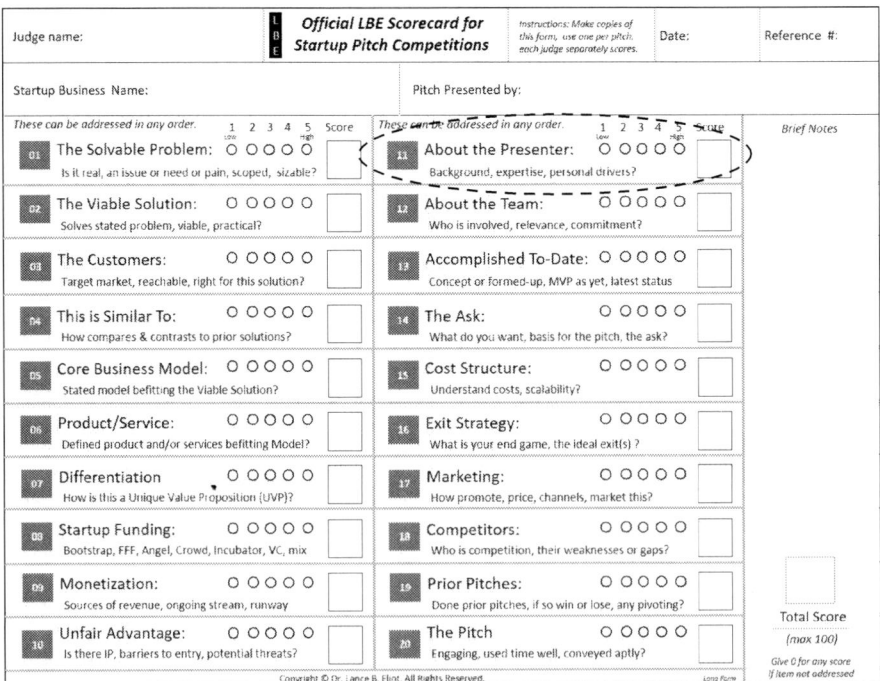

CHAPTER L11
ABOUT THE PRESENTER

What This Is:

You or whomever presents your pitch will be assessed by the judges. I realize that you might think that the judges should only concentrate on the contents of the pitch and the startup itself, but, since the presenter(s) are there making the pitch, they are part and parcel of the assessment. A lousy presenter can sadly undermine the best of startup pitches.

Why Is It Important:

The judges take a hard look at the presenter and naturally assume that the presenter is there as a duly authorized representative of the startup. Usually, it is the founder, but if not the founder than certainly some high ranking officer of the firm and one that is intimately involved in the firm. Assessing a startup also means assessing the people involved in the startup.

Questions You Will be Asked:

o   Did the presenter do a good job presenting the startup?
o   Were they able to use the time allotted effectively?
o   How well did they explain the startup and seem to know it?
o   During Q&A, were answers provided that made sense?
o   Did the presenter have the expertise for this kind of startup?
o   Was there a passion and excitement exhibited?

Typical Scoring Scale:

0 = There was no presenter
1 = The presenter barely was able to convey the startup aspects
2 = Presenter tried but had various problems while presenting
3 = The presenter did a sufficient job of the presentation
4 = Presenter was enthusiastic and knew what they were saying
5 = Incredible presenter that got it done with flair and vibe

CHAPTER L12

ABOUT THE TEAM

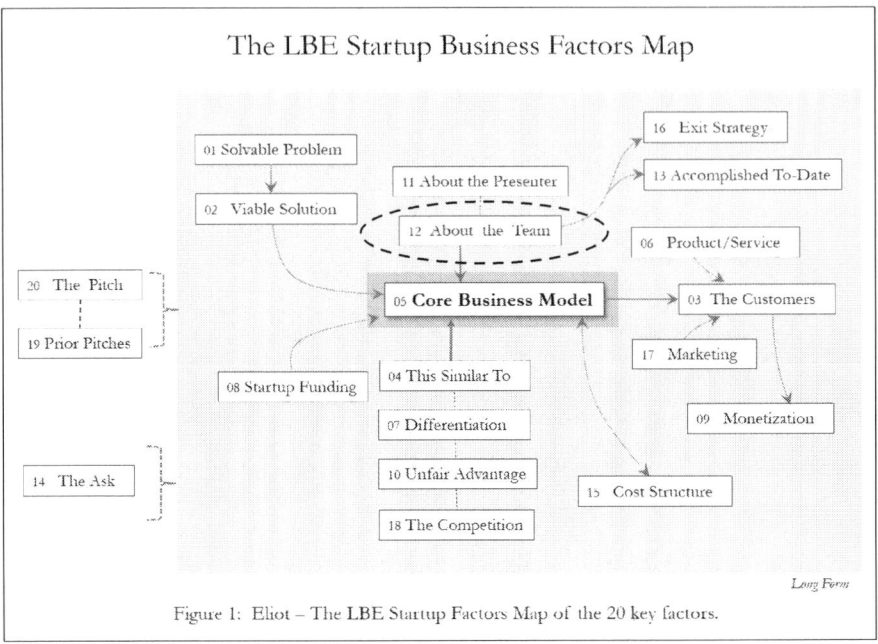

Figure 1: Eliot – The LBE Startup Factors Map of the 20 key factors.

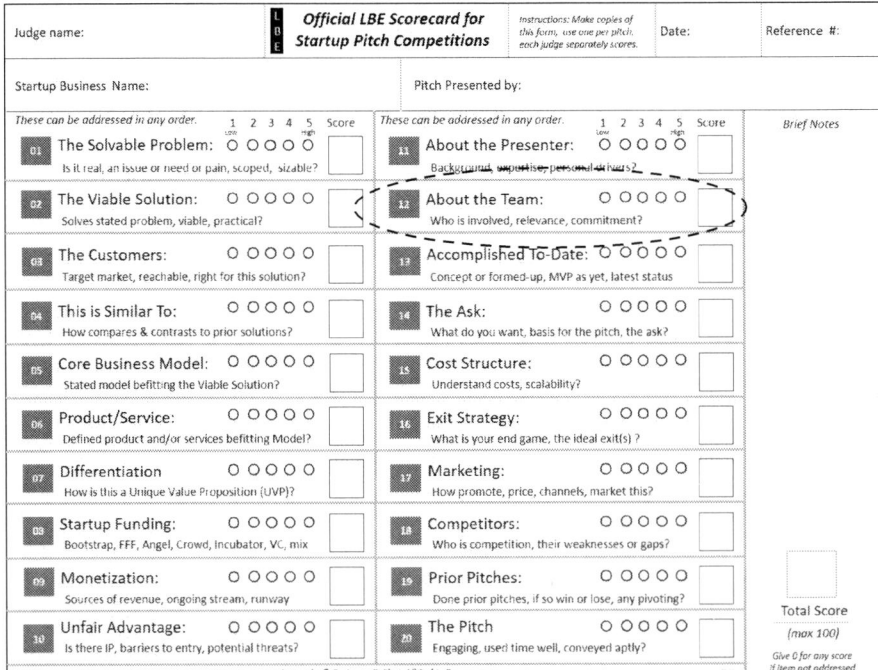

CHAPTER L12

ABOUT THE TEAM

What This Is:

Your startup needs a team. The members of the team are crucial. Suppose you are doing a startup on obesity and are creating a mobile app to aid in weight loss. Having a well-known expert on obesity and weight loss would be advantageous. Having an expert in mobile app development and deployment would be advantageous.

Why Is It Important:

The team that you have assembled will be the ones that make the startup get underway. They must have the right mix of skills and experiences. They must have the commitment to the startup. They must have a passion and interest in the startup. Listing names of people that aren't really involved will get you dinged.

Questions You Will be Asked:

- o Who are the members of your team?
- o What is their profile and relevance to the startup?
- o What commitment have they made to the startup?
- o How do you know these other team members?
- o Have you all worked together before?
- o How much have you now worked together on this startup?
- o What risks are there that the team members might bolt?

Typical Scoring Scale:

- 0 = Did not address the team members topic at all
- 1 = Mentioned the team members vaguely
- 2 = Described the team members but they seem irrelevant
- 3 = Team members were well described and explained
- 4 = Has assembled a strong team that can work together well
- 5 = Top aces together and are working seamlessly

CHAPTER L13
ACCOMPLISHED TO-DATE

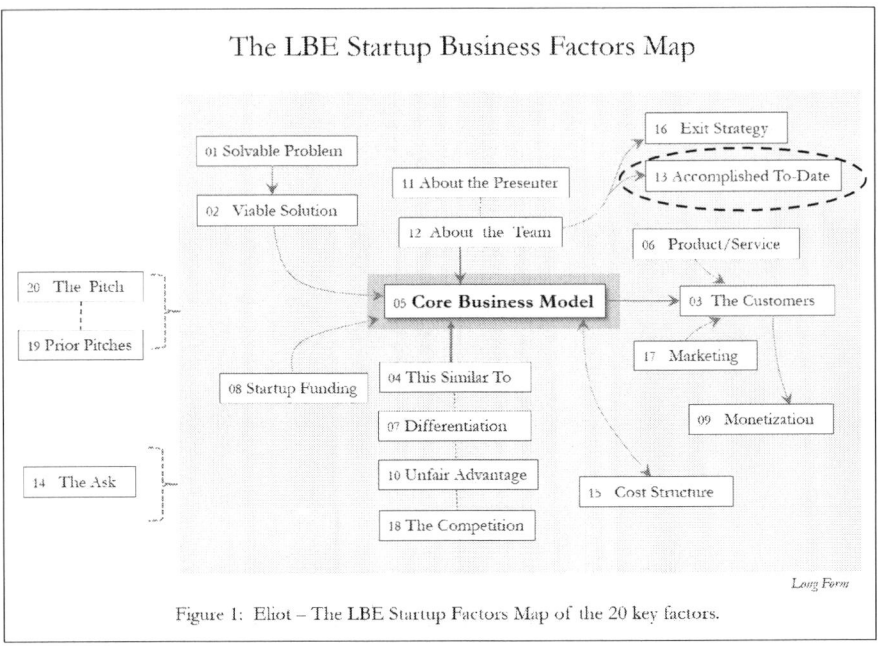

Figure 1: Eliot – The LBE Startup Factors Map of the 20 key factors.

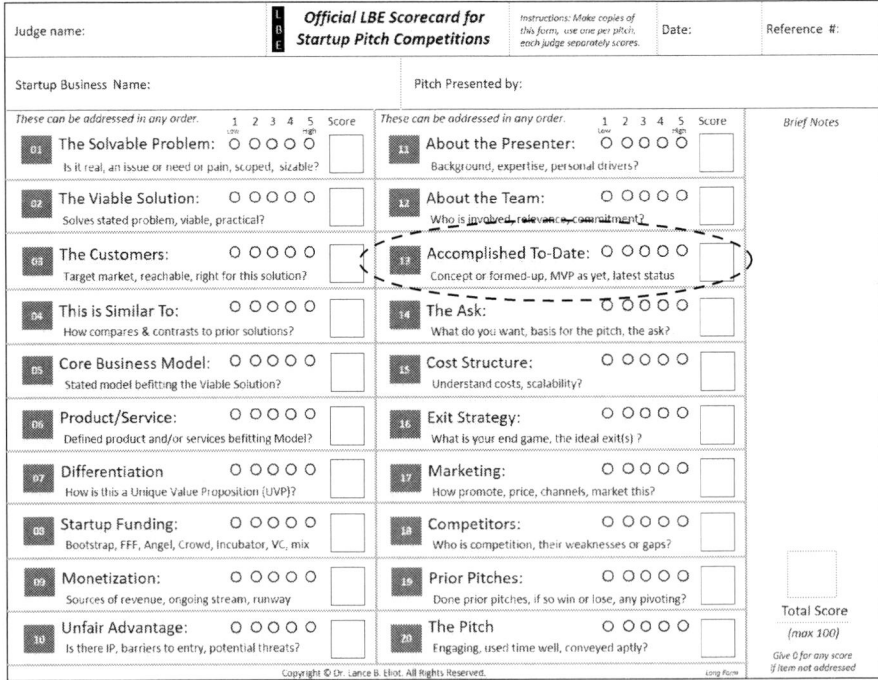

CHAPTER L13
ACCOMPLISHED TO-DATE

What This Is:

Your startup might have already gotten underway and made a lot of progress, which is often referred to as gaining "traction," or it might be still in the concept stage of maturity. When making your pitch, it can be confusing to the judges as to whether you are describing what the startup has done already or indicating what it will be doing in the coming future. Spell out the aspects of what the startup has accomplished to-date and the kind of traction it is proving.

Why Is It Important:

Knowing what the current status of the startup is will aid in others understanding the nature of your ask. If you have already made a lot of accomplishments, perhaps having created a product and started selling it, don't leave that out of your pitch. For one pitch, only during the Q&A did we discover that the startup already had made over a million dollars in revenue and had been selling its product for nearly a year. That's the kind of good news that needs to go front-and-center.

Questions You Will be Asked:

o   What have you done to-date on your startup?
o   What troubles or issues did you confront?
o   Are you as far along at this time as you thought you would be?
o   How much of your funds have you used to accomplish this?
o   In what ways have you adjusted due to progress so far?

Typical Scoring Scale:

0 = Did not address the accomplishments to-date
1 = Mentioned the accomplishments vaguely
2 = Described the accomplishments but it seems insignificant
3 = Accomplishments were described and they are positive
4 = Good accomplishments, adjusting, progressing well
5 = Great accomplishments to-date, amazing progress

CHAPTER L14

THE ASK

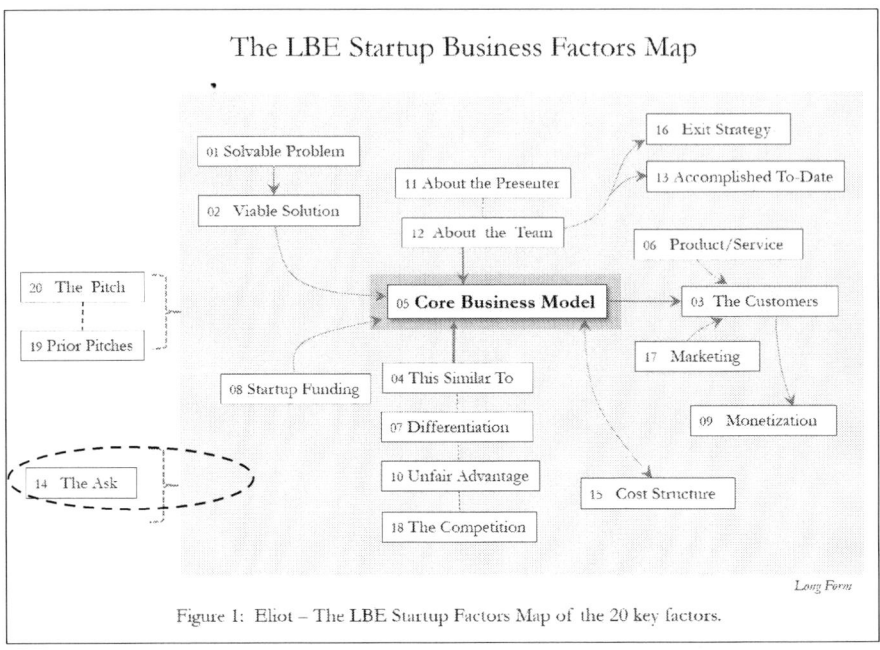

Figure 1: Eliot – The LBE Startup Factors Map of the 20 key factors.

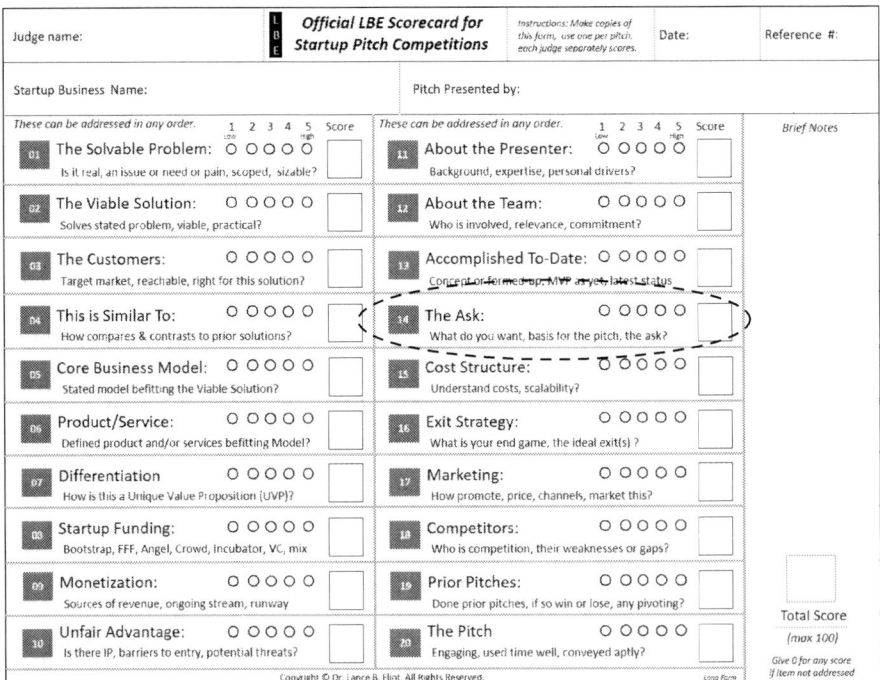

CHAPTER L14
THE ASK

What This Is:

One of the most important aspects of your pitch, and the one aspect that often unbelievably gets omitted, involves asking for what you want to have happen in order to move the startup further forward. I have seen pitches whereby the judges and the investors were all stoked at the startup, and then the founder suddenly finished and sat down. We had no idea what she wanted from us. Big build-up squandered.

Why Is It Important:

You need to say what your ask is. Do you need $50,000 or $500,000 to make it to the next stage? What percentage of your firm will the investor get? How did you arrive at your market cap or value? Do you need mentors or advisers to guide you or open doors? What do you need? It is very revealing to tell your ask, because it then lets the judges know where you are at today and what you believe you need next. Investors in the room will also know whether you are in their ballpark or not. Don't leave us wildly guessing.

Questions You Will be Asked:

o   What is your ask?
o   Why do you believe that your ask is needed?
o   Are you asking for too much? Or, not enough?
o   How can you assure us that you will succeed with the ask?
o   Who else have you told your ask to?

Typical Scoring Scale:

0 = Did not indicate the ask
1 = Mentioned the ask vaguely
2 = Described the ask but it seems off-base of what is needed
3 = Ask was described and it seems valid
4 = Has carefully plotted the ask and will make could use of it
5 = The ask is smart, innovative, and on-target

CHAPTER L15
COST STRUCTURE

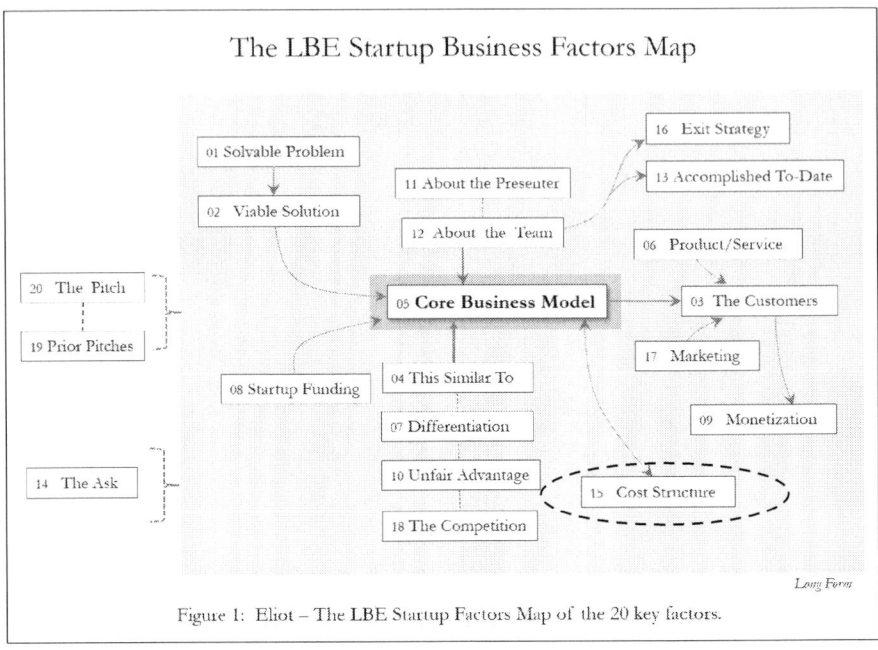

Figure 1: Eliot – The LBE Startup Factors Map of the 20 key factors.

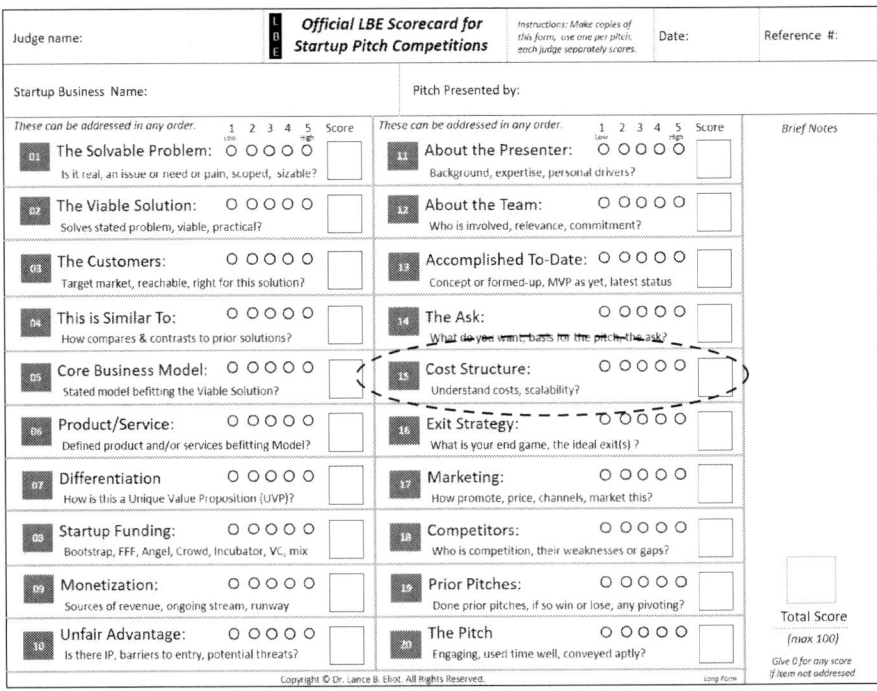

CHAPTER L15
COST STRUCTURE

What This Is:

Those darned costs. Your startup will be burning money like it grows on trees. You need to have a solid understanding of your cost structure. What kinds of fixed costs do you have? What kind of variable costs? Are you aware of the importance of accounting and keeping books? Some startups get themselves into a real mess because the founder has no idea of the costs and where they are being incurred.

Why Is It Important:

Knowing your cost structure is vital for the ongoing health of the startup. Also, once the startup gets further along, the costs are likely to mount. I remember one pitch by a founder that had a frozen food product that was being made by hand. If the food products takes off in the marketplace, what kinds of costs are there going to be? Can the startup scale-up or will hidden costs of today come out to bite you?

Questions You Will be Asked:

o   What is your cost structure?
o   How are you keeping track of your costs?
o   Are you trying to minimize your costs?
o   Will the cost structure inhibit your growth?
o   Are you not incurring enough costs to let the startup grow?

Typical Scoring Scale:

0 = Did not address the cost structure
1 = Mentioned the cost structure vaguely
2 = Described the cost structure but it seems messed-up
3 = Cost structure was described and it seems valid
4 = Understands the cost structure and is managing it quite well
5 = Great at minimizing costs, flexible structure, solid for the future

CHAPTER L16

EXIT STRATEGY

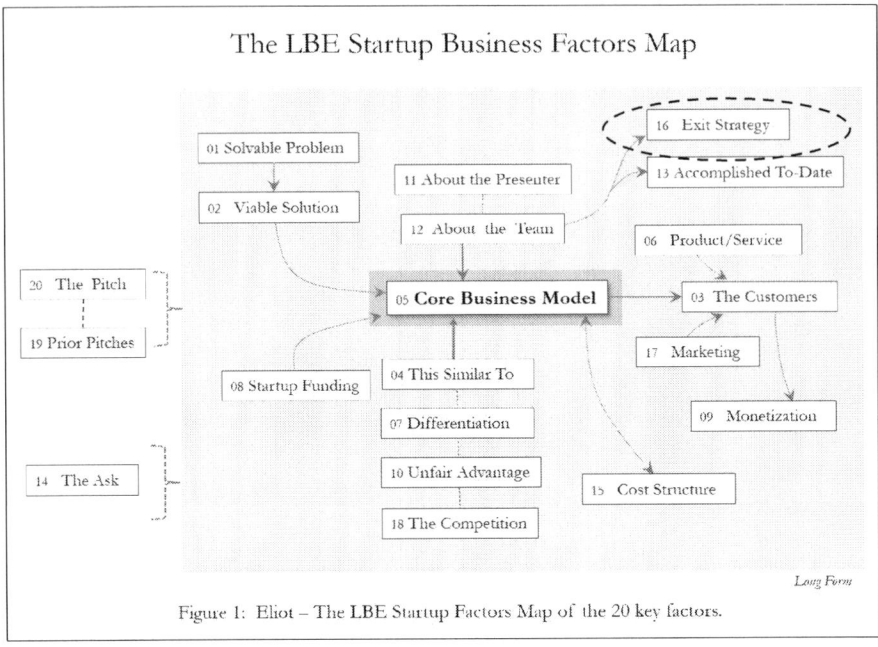

Figure 1: Eliot – The LBE Startup Factors Map of the 20 key factors.

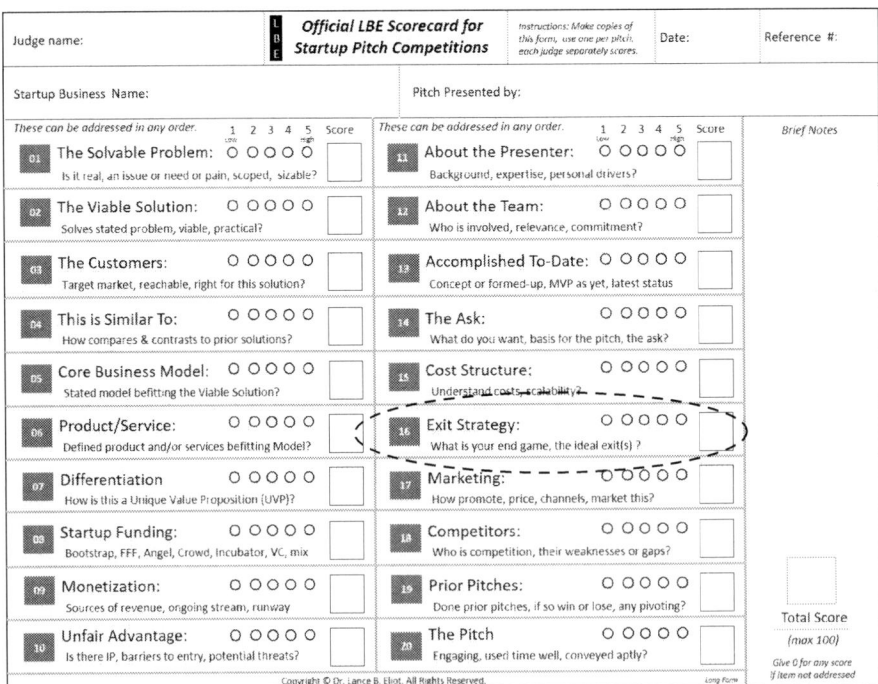

CHAPTER L16
EXIT STRATEGY

What This Is:

> Your startup needs to have an exit strategy. Many founders neglect to think about this and are only looking at the very near-term of the startup. During a pitch, the judges are likely to ask you what the exit strategy is. What is the expectation of the team members? How far down the road do you see the exit? What conditions will bring the exit to fruition?

Why Is It Important:

> Investors want to know when and how you think that there is an exit. The exit point usually generates a payback to investors and the founders. Are you anticipating doing an Initial Public Offering (IPO)? Are you looking toward a buyout? Are you setting up the startup to be acquired? These are important to anyone investing in the firm or that will even help the firm along its journey.

Questions You Will be Asked:

- o   What is your exit strategy?
- o   How realistic is the proposed exit?
- o   When do you envision the exit will occur?
- o   What other firms of a similar nature exited this way?
- o   What is your contingency exit strategy?

Typical Scoring Scale:

- 0 = Did not address the exit strategy
- 1 = Mentioned the exit strategy vaguely
- 2 = Described the exit strategy but it make no sense
- 3 = Exit strategy was described and it seems valid
- 4 = Well-crafted exit strategy that seems strong
- 5 = Exit strategy with contingencies and excellent fit

CHAPTER L17

MARKETING

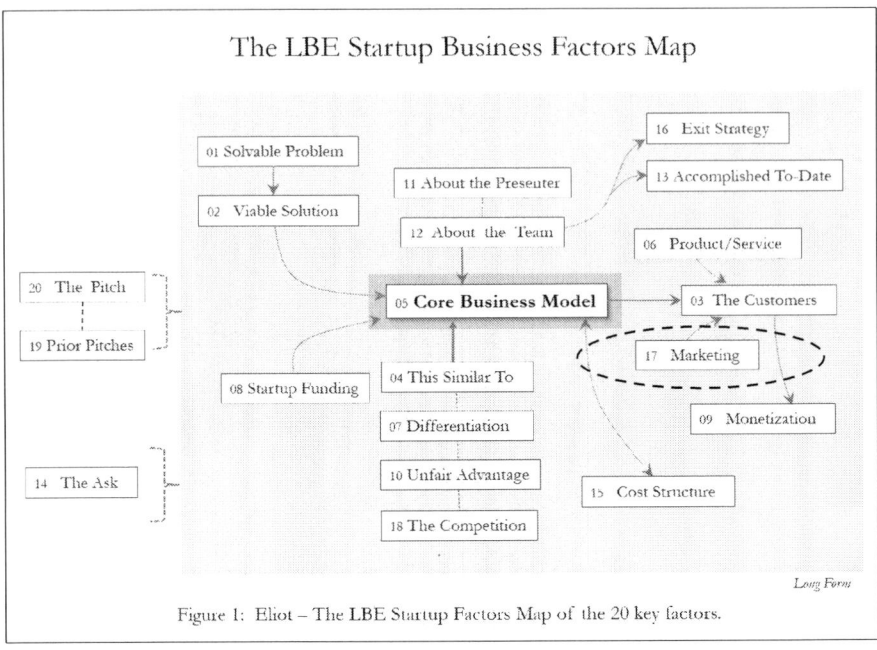

Figure 1: Eliot – The LBE Startup Factors Map of the 20 key factors.

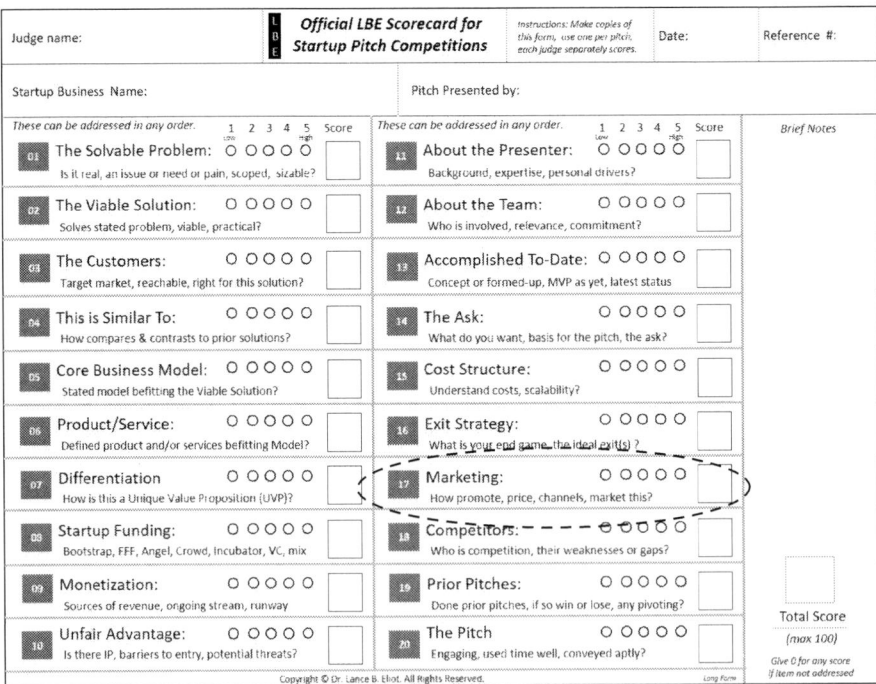

CHAPTER L17
MARKETING

What This Is:

Your startup needs to find a means to get the marketplace aware of what your product or service is. Even if you have the better mousetrap, if no one knows about it, you aren't going to sell it. You need to identify your channels, often referred to as your "Omni-channel approach" that indicates how you will reach your customers, whether by brick-and-mortar stores, online stores, social media, etc.

Why Is It Important:

Knowing the marketing approach tells the judges that you have thought about how to reach your customers, including the cost of customer acquisition. One founder was pitching and when we asked about the cost of acquiring a customer, the founder faltered, told us the number, and we realized that the cost was so high that he would never see any profit. Figure out your product or service pricing, the placement or channel, and devise a marketing strategy.

Questions You Will be Asked:

o   What is your marketing strategy?
o   How do you know it will work?
o   What have you done already in terms of marketing?
o   Indicate the specific channels and why each is valuable to you?
o   What is your cost of acquiring a customer?
o   Who on your team knows marketing?
o
Typical Scoring Scale:

0 = Did not address the marketing strategy
1 = Mentioned the marketing strategy vaguely
2 = Described the marketing strategy but it needs fixing
3 = Marketing strategy was described and it seems valid
4 = Really well understands marketing and has a solid approach
5 = Great at marketing and a true stronghold of the startup

.

CHAPTER L18

COMPETITORS

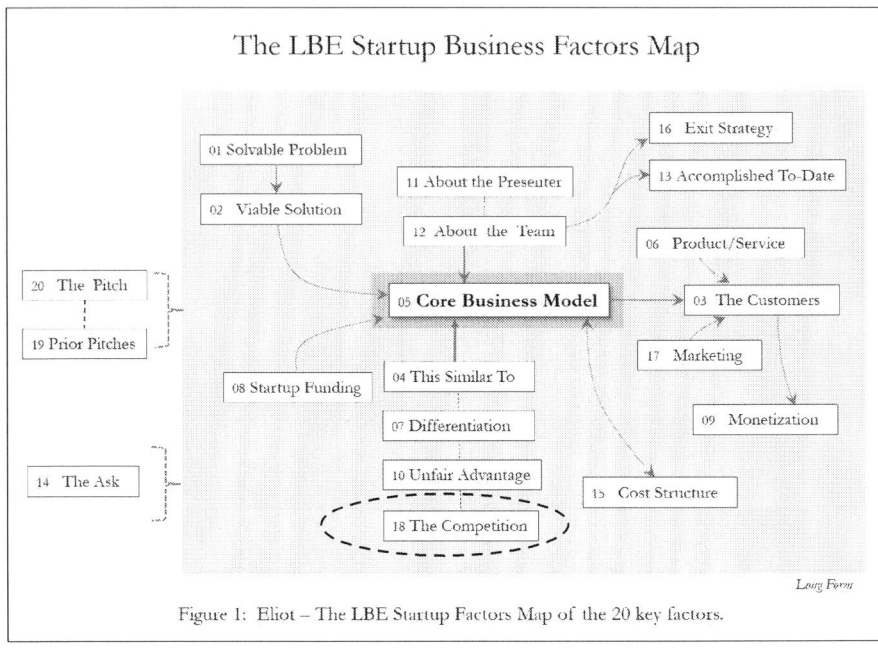

Figure 1: Eliot – The LBE Startup Factors Map of the 20 key factors.

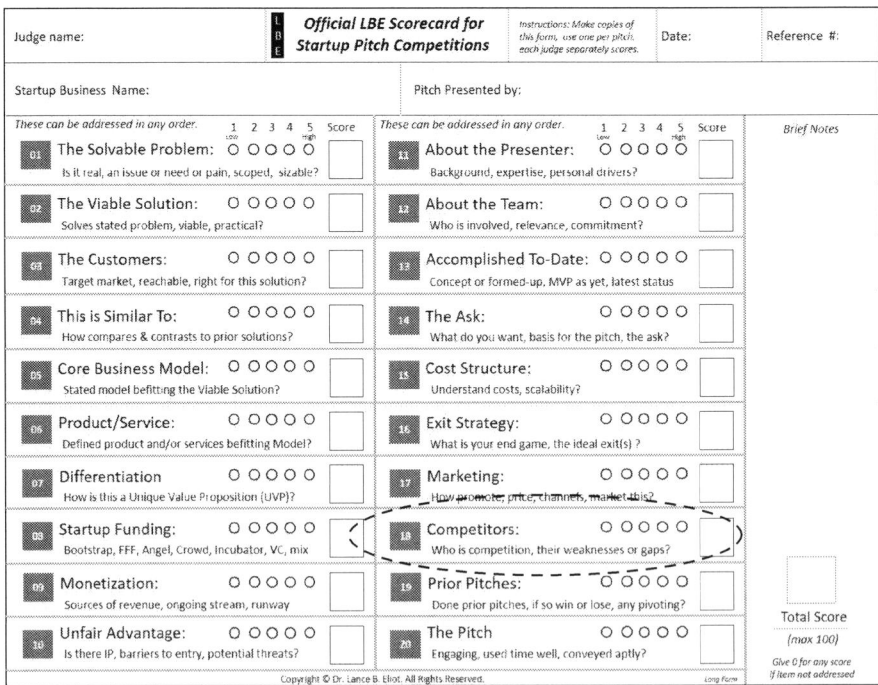

CHAPTER L18

COMPETITORS

What This Is:

> Your startup needs to identify who your competitors are. There will be some competitors that are thorny and will be tough for you to go against, while other competitors might be smaller or just at the periphery of what you are doing. You must know who your competitors are, otherwise your lunch will get eaten by them.

Why Is It Important:

> Your competitors will grab your customers, they will grab your revenue, they will find ways to stop you, they will make roadblocks, they will do whatever they can to keep you out of their turf. They will also enter into your turf, especially if your startup shows that there is a buck to be made. You can't be blind about your competition.

Questions You Will be Asked:

- o Who are your main competitors?
- o What do you know about those competitors?
- o What is your strategy to go against them?
- o How will those competitors try to impinge upon you?
- o What will you do to protect yourself from them?
- o How fierce is your target market in terms of competition?

Typical Scoring Scale:

- 0 = Did not address the competitors at all
- 1 = Mentioned the competitors vaguely
- 2 = Described the competitors but has not done proper research
- 3 = Competitors were described and has a strategy about them
- 4 = Has some insightful ways of dealing with the competition
- 5 = Showed great ways to blow the competition out of the water

CHAPTER L19
PRIOR PITCHES

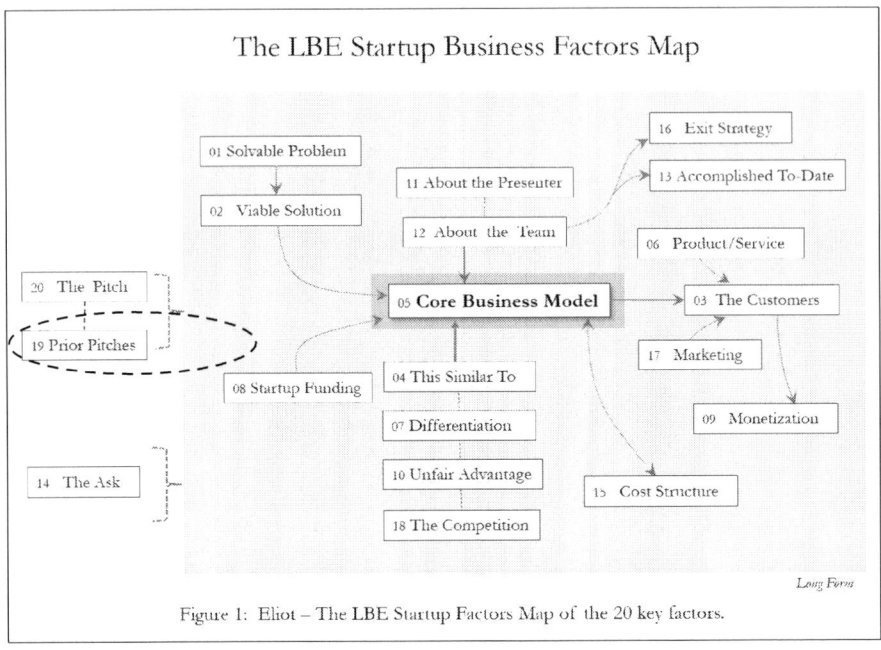

Figure 1: Eliot – The LBE Startup Factors Map of the 20 key factors.

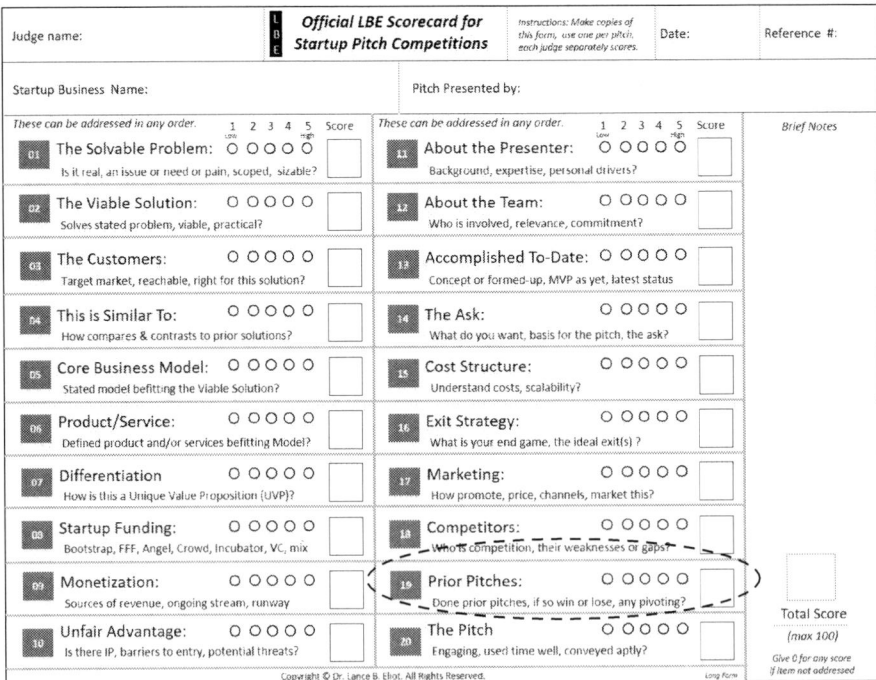

CHAPTER L19
PRIOR PITCHES

What This Is:

> Your startup will likely be involved in making many pitches. The judges want to know who you have pitched to and the results of those pitches. The pitches might be to private groups like a set of angel investors, or it might be pitches at other startup pitch competitions.

Why Is It Important:

> Indicating that you have been making pitches is a good sign that your startup is underway and you realize the value of pitching. Even if you have not won pitches, you can still look good by showing earnest attempts and progressive improvement. If you are pitching excessively and not learning from it, that's a bad sign.

Questions You Will be Asked:

- o Where have you pitched before?
- o Why did you do the pitches?
- o What was the result?
- o What did you learn or gain from those pitches?
- o How do those pitches compare to the one you are doing today?

Typical Scoring Scale:

0 = Did not address whether has done prior pitches or not

1 = Mentioned the prior pitches vaguely

2 = Described the prior pitches but did not learn anything from it

3 = Prior pitches were described and good adjustments

4 = Has made solid prior pitches, almost won some, progressing

5 = Winner at prior pitches, gaining reputation as a strong startup

CHAPTER L20
THE PITCH

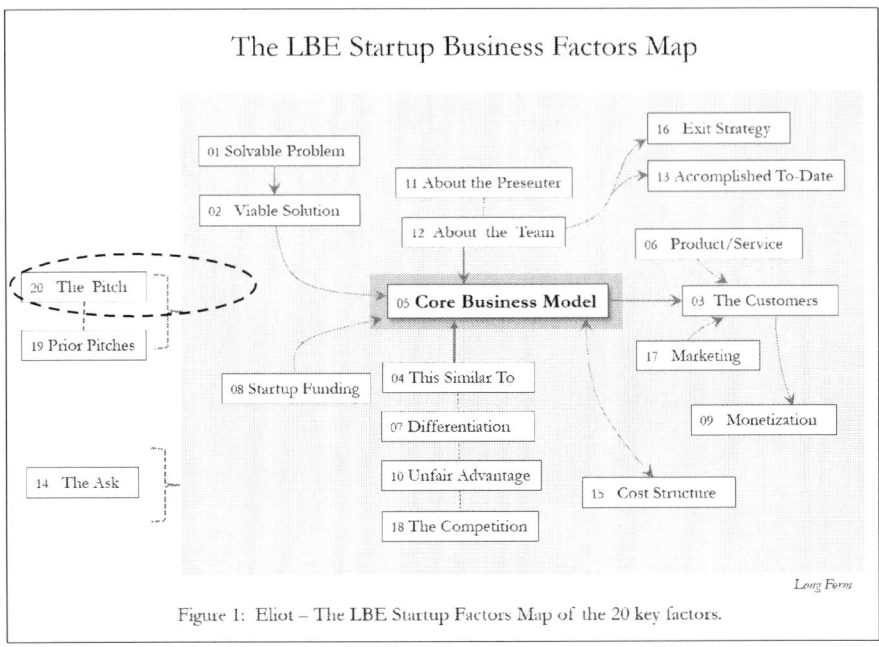

Figure 1: Eliot – The LBE Startup Factors Map of the 20 key factors.

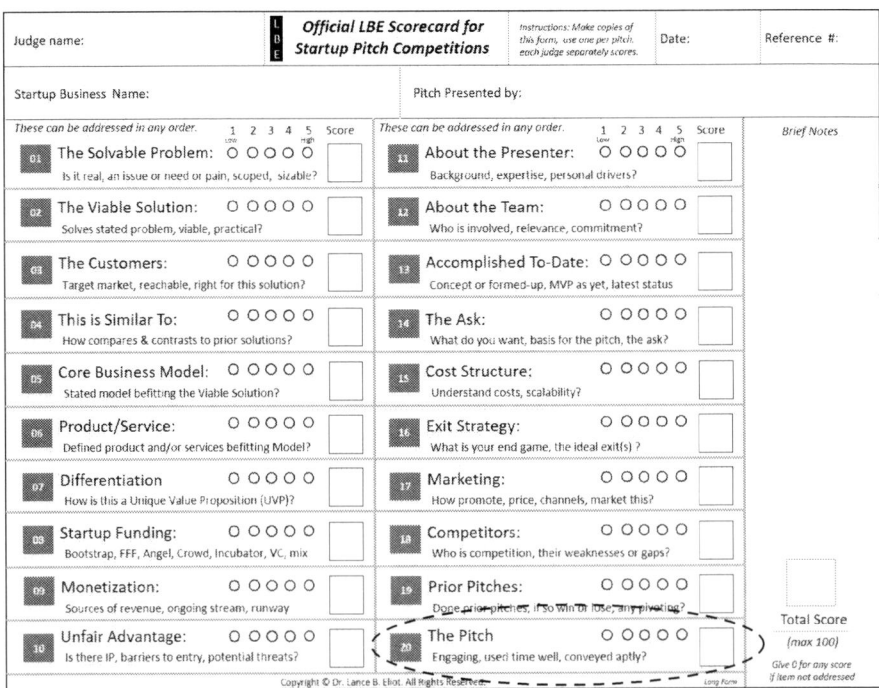

CHAPTER L20
THE PITCH

What This Is:

> Your startup is assessed on how good or lousy your pitch was. Stepping aside of the presenter (which was covered in L11), this is a focus on the pitch itself. Was the pitch complete? Was the pitch expressive? Did the pitch portray your startup in a positive way?

Why Is It Important:

> The pitch itself is an earmark of what your brand and image is. If you have a scrambled pitch, it suggests that your firm is equally scrambled. A cogent and on-target pitch is more believable and creates greater confidence in the startup and the team of the startup. Some say it is unfair to judge a startup by the pitch, and that instead the startup should be considered separately of the pitch. This is hard to separate out because all that the judges have to assess is whatever was conveyed as a result of the pitch.

Questions You Will be Asked:

- o Was the pitch well prepared and appropriately rehearsed?
- o Did it seem professional and expressive?
- o Was the coverage of the elements sufficient?
- o Were there any gaps or glaring omissions?
- o Did the pitch allot time to the right parts of the pitch?
- o Was there a "wow!" factor that made the pitch memorable?

Typical Scoring Scale:

0 = There was no pitch

1 = The pitch was a mess

2 = The pitch occurred, some of it was sensible, but needs help

3 = Pitch was good

4 = Pitch went beyond good and was impressive

5 = Remarkable pitch and had a strong "wow!" factor to it

CONCLUSION
& FINAL ADVICE

CONCLUSION & FINAL ADVICE

You are now ready to participate in a startup pitch competition. If you have carefully and thoughtfully considered the aspects that I have identified in this book, you are way ahead of most other participants. I would dare say you are now in the 1% that cares enough about doing a startup pitch competition that you have opted to study up and get yourself informed. I am confident this will show itself as you do a pitch.

For some founders, doing any kind of pitch can be seemingly hard for them to do. Having lived with their startup, they find it difficult to express what they are trying to do and what they are seeking to achieve. They know it in their heart and head, but sometimes have a rough time telling others about it. They are often the type of person that "wants to get on with the hard work of growing the business" and perceives that making pitches is somehow distracting or merely an irritating tangent.

Unless you can bankroll the firm entirely by yourself or with family and friends, the odds are high that you will need to make a pitch for funding. Getting funding can be enhanced by having done startup pitch competitions for the practice of pitching, and also if you win then you can use that to impress investors that your startup is more than a pipedream that only you believe in. You can say that a panel of judges, making sure to list their qualifications, anointed your startup as qualified and declared your startup as heads above other startups.

Some founders are shy about pitching and want their startup to miraculously sell itself. Or, they are modest and don't want to brag about themselves. For them, I say get out of your shell and get used to pitching. In terms of bragging, you have every right to brag, since doing a startup is gutsy and worthy of bragging about. Meanwhile, there are some founders that are more like used car salespersons and will pitch anywhere at any time to anyone. For them, I urge you to make sure that you have something useful to brag about and don't let your sales gusto overshadow the aspect that the informed judges will want to also know the substance of the startup.

Let me close by quoting a famous Latin phrase: *Carthago delenda est* (from Ancient Rome; absolutely support your ideas). Please do so!

APPENDIX

APPENDIX A

TEACHING WITH THIS MATERIAL

The material in this book can be readily used either as a supplemental to other content for a class, or it can also be used as a core set of textbook material for a specialized class. Classes where this material is most likely used include any classes at the college or university level that want to augment the class by offering thought provoking and educational essays about startups and entrepreneurship.

In particular, here are some aspects for class use:

o   <u>Startups</u>. Studying business startups and what the elements of a startup consist of.

o   <u>Entrepreneurship</u>. Exploring what founders need to know and do, in order to get their startup underway and how they need to pitch their startup.

o   <u>Business</u>. Focusing on business aspects for founders that might not have a business background per se, and perhaps come from some other specialty and are trying to break into being a business person.

Specialized classes at the undergraduate and graduate level can also make use of this material. A course in an engineering department that is about startups could find this book handy. Also, an MBA-seminar class at the graduate level on entrepreneurship is one such example of how this material has been used.

For each chapter, consider whether you think the chapter provides material relevant to your course topic. There is plenty of opportunity to get the students thinking about the topic and force them to decide whether they agree or disagree with the points offered and positions taken. I would also encourage you to have the students do additional research beyond the chapter material presented (I provide next some suggested assignments they can do).

RESEARCH ASSIGNMENTS ON THESE TOPICS

Your students can readily find a plethora of background material on these topics, doing so in the usual business publications such as the Harvard Business Review, Forbes, Fortune, WSJ, and the like.

Here are some suggestions of homework or projects that you could assign to students:

a) <u>Assignment for Startups topic</u>: Research and prepare a paper and a presentation on startups and particularly the topic of pitches. The paper should cite at least 3 reputable sources and analyze how startup pitches are portrayed by those sources. Compare and contrast to what has been stated in this book.

b) <u>Assignment for the Entrepreneurship topic</u>: Research and prepare a paper and a presentation on business founders and entrepreneurs. Cite at least 3 reputable sources and analyze the characterizations. Compare and contrast to what has been stated in this book.

c) <u>Assignment for the Business topic</u>: Research and prepare a paper and a presentation on businesses and business trends. What is hot, and what is not? Cite at least 3 reputable sources. Compare and contrast to the depictions in this book.

d) <u>Assignment to do a Startup Pitch</u>: Have the students make pitches as though they were at a startup pitch competition. Use the scorecards to have the other students serve as judges.

You can certainly adjust the aforementioned assignments to fit to your particular needs and the class structure. You'll notice that I ask for 3 reputable cited sources for the paper writing based assignments. I usually steer students toward "reputable" publications, since otherwise they will cite some oddball source that has no credentials other than that they happened to write something and post it onto the Internet. You can define "reputable" in whatever way you prefer, for example some faculty think Wikipedia is not reputable while others believe it is reputable and allow students to cite it.

The reason that I usually ask for at least 3 citations is that if the student only does one or two citations they usually settle on whatever they happened to find the fastest. By requiring three citations, it usually seems to force them to look around, explore, and end-up probably finding five or more, and then whittling it down to 3 that they will actually use.

I have not specified the length of their papers, and leave that to you to tell the students what you prefer. For each of those assignments, you could end-up with a short one to two pager, or you could do a dissertation length paper. Base the length on whatever best fits for your class, and the credit amount of the assignment within the context of the other grading metrics you'll be using for the class.

I mention in the assignments that they are to do a paper and prepare a presentation. I usually try to get students to present their work. This is a good practice for what they will do in the business world. Most of the time, they will be required to prepare an analysis and present it. If you don't have the class time or inclination to have the students present, then you can of course cut out the aspect of them putting together a presentation.

If you want to point students toward highly ranked journals in business, here's a list of the top journals as reported by *Financial Times* (this list changes year to year, plus you might disagree with how they ranked them):

    i.   Academy of Management Journal

    ii.   Academy of Management Review

    iii.   Accounting, Organizations and Society

    iv.   Administrative Science Quarterly

    v.   American Economic Review

    vi.   Entrepreneurship Theory and Practice

    vii.   Harvard Business Review

    viii.   Human Resource Management

    ix.   Information Systems Research

GUIDE TO USING THE CHAPTERS

For each of the chapters, I provide next some various ways to use the chapter material. You can assign the tasks as individual homework assignments, or the tasks can be used with team projects for the class. You can easily layout a series of assignments, such as indicating that the students are to do item "a" below for say Chapter 1, then "b" for the next chapter of the book, and so on.

a) What is the main point of the chapter and describe in your own words the significance of the topic,

b) Identify at least two aspects in the chapter that you agree with, and support your concurrence by providing at least one other outside researched item as support; make sure to explain your basis for disagreeing with the aspects,

c) Identify at least two aspects in the chapter that you disagree with, and support your disagreement by providing at least one other outside researched item as support; make sure to explain your basis for disagreeing with the aspects,

d) Find an aspect that was not covered in the chapter, doing so by conducting outside research, and then explain how that aspect ties into the chapter and what significance it brings to the topic,

e) Interview an business leader in industry about the topic of the chapter, collect from them their thoughts and opinions, and readdress the chapter by citing your source and how they compared and contrasted to the material,

f) Interview a relevant academic professor or researcher in a college or university about the topic of the chapter, collect from them their thoughts and opinions, and readdress the chapter by citing your source and how they compared and contrasted to the material,

g) Try to update a chapter by finding out the latest on the topic, and ascertain whether the issue or topic has now been solved or whether it is still being addressed, explain what you come up with,

h) Have the students role play as a business leader and ask them to consider the chapter material in light of being a business leader, and explain what they would say or comment in that capacity,

i) Have the students role play as the founder of a start-up and ask them to consider the chapter material in light of being an entrepreneur, and explain what they would say or comment in that capacity,

j) For students that work in a business, have the student describe how the aspects of this book takes place in their business and whether the issue or topic of the chapter is relevant to their firm or not, and say why,

k) Make use of case studies, such as a relevant case study from the Harvard Business Review library, and analyze the case from the perspective of this book and make use of the chapter material as a means to do so.

The above are all ways in which you can get the students of your class involved in considering the material of a given chapter. You could mix things up by having one of those above assignments per each week, covering the chapters over the course of the semester or quarter.

As a reminder, here are the chapters of the book and you can cherry pick whichever chapters you find most valued for your particular class:

<u>Chapter Title</u>

1	Why do a Startup Pitch Competition
2	What Happens at a Startup Pitch Competition
3	The Pitch Judges and How They Think
4	Use the LBE Scorecard as Your Guide
5	Self-Diagnosing Your Startup Via LBE Scorecard
6	Falsehoods about Your Pitch Approach
L1	The Solvable Problem
L2	The Viable Solution
L3	The Customers
L4	This Is Similar To
L5	Core Business Model
L6	Product/Service
L7	Differentiation
L8	Startup Funding
L9	Monetization
L10	Unfair Advantage
L11	About the Presenter
L12	About the Team
L13	Accomplished To-Date
L14	The Ask
L15	Cost Structure
L16	Exit Strategy
L17	Marketing
L18	Competitors
L19	Prior Pitches
L20	The Pitch

I also include on the next pages the key diagrams regarding the scorecard. These are handy tools to be used for teaching purposes.

The LBE Startup Business Factors Map

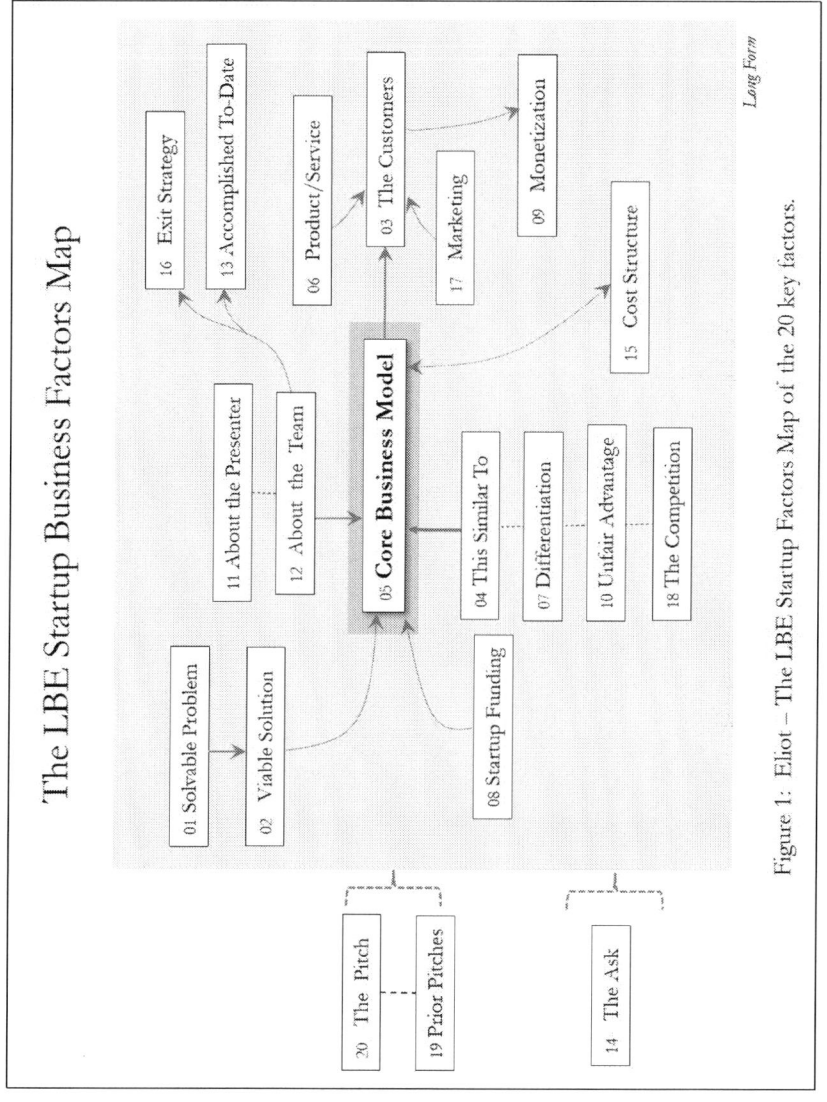

Figure 1: Eliot – The LBE Startup Factors Map of the 20 key factors.

LBE | **Official LBE Scorecard for Startup Pitch Competitions**

Instructions: Make copies of this form, use one per pitch, each judge: separately scores.

Judge name: Date: Reference #:

Startup Business Name:

Pitch Presented by:

These can be addressed in any order.

	1 Low	2	3	4	5 High	Score			1 Low	2	3	4	5 High	Score
01 **The Solvable Problem:** Is it real, an issue or need or pain, scoped, sizable?	O	O	O	O	O		11 **About the Presenter:** Background, expertise, personal drivers?		O	O	O	O	O	
02 **The Viable Solution:** Solves stated problem, viable, practical?	O	O	O	O	O		12 **About the Team:** Who is involved, relevance, commitment?		O	O	O	O	O	
03 **The Customers:** Target market, reachable, right for this solution?	O	O	O	O	O		13 **Accomplished To-Date:** Concept or formed-up, MVP as yet, latest status		O	O	O	O	O	
04 **This is Similar To:** How compares & contrasts to prior solutions?	O	O	O	O	O		14 **The Ask:** What do you want, basis for the pitch, the ask?		O	O	O	O	O	
05 **Core Business Model:** Stated model befitting the Viable Solution?	O	O	O	O	O		15 **Cost Structure:** Understand costs, scalability?		O	O	O	O	O	
06 **Product/Service:** Defined product and/or services befitting Model?	O	O	O	O	O		16 **Exit Strategy:** What is your end game, the ideal exit(s) ?		O	O	O	O	O	
07 **Differentiation:** How is this a Unique Value Proposition (UVP)?	O	O	O	O	O		17 **Marketing:** How promote, price, channels, market this?		O	O	O	O	O	
08 **Startup Funding:** Bootstrap, FFF, Angel, Crowd, Incubator, VC, mix	O	O	O	O	O		18 **Competitors:** Who is competition, their weaknesses or gaps?		O	O	O	O	O	
09 **Monetization:** Sources of revenue, ongoing stream, runway	O	O	O	O	O		19 **Prior Pitches:** Done prior pitches, if so win or lose, any pivoting?		O	O	O	O	O	
10 **Unfair Advantage:** Is there IP, barriers to entry, potential threats?	O	O	O	O	O		20 **The Pitch:** Engaging, used time well, conveyed aptly?		O	O	O	O	O	

Brief Notes

Total Score (max 100)

Give 0 for any score if item not addressed.

Long Form

.

* Pitch in Silicon Beach - Example *

Official LBE Scorecard for Startup Pitch Competitions

Instructions: Make copies of this form, use one per pitch, each judge separately scores.

Judge name: Lance Eliot   Date: 9/30   Reference #: 22

Startup Business Name: SnapHat

Pitch Presented by: Michael Spruce

These can be addressed in any order.

		low 1	2	3	4	5 high	Score
01	**The Solvable Problem:** Is it real, an issue or need or pain, scoped, sizable?	O	O	O	⊗	O	4
02	**The Viable Solution:** Solves stated problem, viable, practical?	O	O	O	⊗	O	4
03	**The Customers:** Target market, reachable, right for this solution?	O	O	⊗	O	O	3
04	**This is Similar To:** Snapchat	O	O	⊗	O	O	3
05	**Core Business Model:** Stated model befitting the Viable Solution?	O	O	O	⊗	O	4
06	**Product/Service:** Defined product and/or services befitting Model?	O	O	O	⊗	O	4
07	**Differentiation**	O	⊗	O	O	O	2
08	**Startup Funding:** $250K	O	O	O	O	⊗	5
09	**Monetization:** Not likely	O	⊗	O	O	O	2
10	**Unfair Advantage:**	⊗	O	O	O	O	1

These can be addressed in any order.

		low 1	2	3	4	5 high	Score	Brief Notes
11	**About the Presenter:** Background, expertise, personal drivers?	O	O	O	⊗	O	4	Pressing
12	**About the Team:** Who is involved, relevance, commitment?	O	O	⊗	O	O	3	believes in his startup
13	**Accomplished To-Date:** Concept or formed-up, MVP as yet, latest status	O	O	O	⊗	O	4	But this has been done before. No standout.
14	**The Ask:** What do you want, basis for the pitch, the ask?	O	⊗	O	O	O	2	
15	**Cost Structure:** Understand costs, scalability?	⊗	O	O	O	O	0	
16	**Exit Strategy:** What is your end game, the ideal exit(s)?	O	⊗	O	O	O	2	Consider a pivot. Find UVP.
17	**Marketing:** How promote, price, channels, market this?	O	⊗	O	O	O	2	
18	**Competitors:** Who is competition, their weaknesses or gaps?	O	O	O	⊗	O	4	
19	**Prior Pitches:** Done prior pitches, if so win or lose, any pivoting?	O	O	O	⊗	O	4	
20	**The Pitch** Engaging, used time well, conveyed aptly?	O	O	O	⊗	O	4	

Total Score (max 100): 61

Give 0 for any score if item not addressed

Copyright © Dr. Lance B. Eliot. All Rights Reserved.

181

L B E — Official LBE Scorecard for Startup Pitch Competitions

Judge name:

Instructions: Make copies of this form, use one per pitch, each judge separately scores.

Date:

Reference #:

Startup Business Name:

Pitch Presented by:

Judge Notes

These can be addressed in any order.

| | 1 | 2 | 3 | 4 | 5 | Score |
| | Low | | | | High | |

01 The Solvable Problem: ○ ○ ○ ○ ○
Is it real, an issue or need or pain, scoped, sizable?

02 The Viable Solution: ○ ○ ○ ○ ○
Solves stated problem, viable, practical?

05 Core Business Model: ○ ○ ○ ○ ○
Stated model befitting the Viable Solution?

08 Startup Funding: ○ ○ ○ ○ ○
Bootstrap, FFF, Angel, Crowd, Incubator, VC, mix

12 About the Team: ○ ○ ○ ○ ○
Who is involved, relevance, commitment?

14 The Ask: ○ ○ ○ ○ ○
What do you want, basis for the pitch, the ask?

Other Factors

03 The Customers	13 Accomplished To-Date
04 This is Similar To	15 Cost Structure
06 Product/Service	16 Exit Strategy
07 Differentiation	17 Marketing
09 Monetization	18 Competitors
10 Unfair Advantage	19 Prior Pitches
11 About the Presenter	20 The Pitch

Total Score
(max 30)
Give 0 for any score
if item not addressed

Short Form

ABOUT THE AUTHOR

Dr. Lance B. Eliot, MBA, PhD is known as a Thought Leader in business, and has over twenty years of industry experience, including serving as a corporate officer in a billion dollar firm, and was a Partner in a major executive services firm. He is also a serial entrepreneur having founded, ran, and sold several high-tech related businesses. He previously hosted the popular radio show *Technotrends* that was also available on American Airlines flights via their in-flight audio program. Author or co-author of five books and over 300 articles, he has made appearances on CNN, and has been a frequent speaker at industry conferences.

A former professor at the University of Southern California (USC), he founded and led an innovative research lab on Artificial Intelligence in Business. He also previously served on the faculty of the University of California Los Angeles (UCLA), and was a visiting professor at other major universities. He was elected to the International Board of the Society for Information Management (SIM), a prestigious association of over 3,000 high-tech executives worldwide.

He has performed extensive community service, including serving as Senior Science Adviser to the Vice Chair of the Congressional Committee on Science & Technology. He has served on the Board of the OC Science & Engineering Fair (OCSEF), where he is also has been a Grand Sweepstakes judge, and likewise served as a judge for the Intel International SEF (ISEF). He served as the Vice Chair of the Association for Computing Machinery (ACM) Chapter, a prestigious association of computer scientists. Dr. Eliot has been a shark tank judge for the USC Mark Stevens Center for Innovation on start-up pitch competitions, and served as a mentor for several incubators and accelerators in Silicon Valley and Silicon Beach. He serves on several Boards and Committees at USC, including the Marshall Alumni Association (MAA) Board for Los Angeles and Orange County in Southern California.

Dr. Eliot holds a PhD from USC, MBA, and Bachelor's in Computer Science, and earned the CDP, CCP, CSP, CDE, and CISA certifications. Born and raised in Southern California, and having traveled and lived internationally, he enjoys scuba diving, surfing, and sailing.

ADDENDUM

How to Win a Startup Pitch Competition

*Successful Insights from a
Topnotch Judge for Boosting Your Startup*

By
Dr. Lance B. Eliot, MBA, PhD

———

For supplemental materials of this book, visit:
www.lance-blog.com

For special orders of this book, contact:
LBE Press Publishing
Email: LBE.Press.Publishing@gmail.com

Printed in Great Britain
by Amazon

49762891R00110